WITH CHARITY
TOWARD NONE

WITH CHARITY TOWARD NONE

A Fond Look at Misanthropy

FLORENCE KING

ST. MARTIN'S PRESS
NEW YORK

Design by Glen M. Edelstein

Library of Congress Cataloging-in-Publication Data
King, Florence.
    With charity toward none : a fond look at misanthropy / Florence
King
      p. cm.
    ISBN 0-312-07124-8
    1. Misanthrophy—Humor. 2. Charity—Humor. I. Title.
PN6231.M59K56 1992
814'.54—dc20   91-34803
                                                         CIP

First Edition: March 1992

10 9 8 7 6 5 4 3 2 1

for Tom McCormack, Cal Morgan, and Mel Berger

"I hate and despise the animal called Mankind but I like the occasional Tom, Dick, and Harry."—Jonathan Swift

CONTENTS

ACKNOWLEDGMENTS

He travels fastest who travels alone, and that goes double for she, but sometimes it isn't possible. The following individuals—all of whom, let me emphasize, are entirely normal—traveled a few steps with me and therefore have my gratitude.

Patricia O'Toole, author of the delightful group biography, *The Five of Hearts: An Intimate Portrait of Henry Adams and His Friends, 1880–1918,* for listening to my thoughts on Henry and sharing some of hers with me.

John Siman, professor of classics at Johns Hopkins University, for checking my rusty Latin.

The staff of the Central Rappahannock Regional Library: Fredericksburg Branch, which mouthful is known locally as "the lah-berry," for the reserves, inter-library loans, and copying they did for me. Ginger Burke, Ellen Hagan, Betty Hume, Catherine Luce, Mildred Vittoria, Judith Webster, Mary Storm Westbrook, E. Sue Willis, and Carmela Ballato Witzke all went out

ACKNOWLEDGMENTS

of their way to help me and delivered with efficiency and prompt-ness—and friendliness. You would have to visit this library to believe it: it has the ambience of a neighborhood speakeasy.

My special thanks go to another library staff member, Diane Deuel, who is also my downstairs neighbor. When I had the flu and couldn't go out, Diane very graciously brought inter-library loans home for me and took them back. Moreover—and this is not for publication—she also sneaked back a reference book that I accidentally walked off with. We're still trying to figure out why the alarm didn't go off.

WITH CHARITY
TOWARD NONE

AUTHOR'S NOTE

From *The American Heritage Dictionary: "misanthrope* also *misanthropist* n. A person who hates or scorns mankind. [Fr. < Gk. *misanthropos,* hating mankind: *misein,* to hate + *anthropos,* man.]"

Firsthand, behind-the-scenes information is the kind America likes. Not unmindful of other portions of the equine anatomy, we are the land of the horse's mouth. Alcoholics write books about alcoholism, drug addicts write books about drug addiction, brothel keepers write books about brothel keeping, so I have written a book about misanthropy.

As with repressed Victorians and sex, friendly Americans harbor a secret fascination for the forbidden subject of misanthropy. It reared its head when I told certain people that I was writing this book. Their first response was a hungry-sounding "Ohhh," followed by eager suggestions of whom to put in it.

1

The name proffered most often by intellectual men was Franz Kafka, accompanied by a supporting quotation that they all seem to have underlined: "Nervous states of the worst sort control me without pause. Everything that is not literature bores me and I hate it. I lack all aptitude for family life."

My own favorite Kafkaisms are "A friendship without disruption of one's daily life is unthinkable," and "All that I have accomplished is the result of being alone." As heartwarming as these sentiments are, Kafka's life suggests that his real problem was not so much misanthropy as emotional pulverization by a misanthropic father. According to Franz, the elder Kafka possessed "a knowledge of people and a distrust of most of them," and manifested "aloofness, self-confidence and dissatisfaction with everyone else."

Kafka's free-floating guilt included guilt over his unsociable nature, which he tried to change—something no self-respecting misanthrope would ever do. As a student he took on what we would call extracurricular activities, joining political clubs and even a séance. But despite interesting associates that included Max Brod and Franz Werfel, Kafka never felt comfortable in groups. Writes Louis Untermeyer: "After an hour of talk his nerves would give way, his lips would twitch, his extraordinary black eyes would burn, and he would be racked with headaches."

I know the feeling well, but it is not misanthropy in the strict sense. It is what comes over a touring writer who is too tired to hate. Kafka's whole life was a book tour, which is another way of saying that he was temporarily haunted on a permanent basis. It takes energy to be a misanthrope but Kafka was so overwhelmed by people that he had no strength left to hate them.

My consultants recommended several nihilists and existentialists but I rejected them all. A black turtleneck sweater does not a misanthrope make. Nihilists and existentialists tend to be bohemians, who invariably run in packs; despite their alienated stance they have always struck me as a sociable lot who surround themselves with people because they are forever saying "Nothing matters," and they need someone to say it to.

I have also eliminated pessimists and fatalists such as Oswald Spengler and T.S. Eliot. If we take as one definition of a misanthrope, "Someone who does not suffer fools and likes to see fools suffer," we realize at once that we are dealing with an individual who has something to look forward to. Misanthropes have the "vision thing" down pat. Anticipating the spectacle of seeing fools suffer makes us wake up in the morning with a song in our hearts, even when the suffering fool is an American president with the power to drag us all down with him. A misanthropic Philistine no doubt would have said, "Hey, wouldn't it be a gas if we could get this guy Samson to come over to the temple?" No matter what wastelands we must endure, our motto is: *It was worth it.*

Every woman who volunteered names recommended Dorothy Parker, but she is not to be found herein. A romantic masquerading as a cynic, Parker hated to be alone, and attempted suicide several times after broken romances. Misanthropes love to be alone, and our attitude toward broken romances is the flip side of America's favorite maxim: "A lover is a stranger you haven't met yet."

One woman suggested Jane Austen based on the quotation: "I do not want people to be agreeable, as it saves me the trouble of liking them." This remark bespeaks a standard occupational hazard in an otherwise outgoing lady. Writers are more interested in people than fond of them; life is a laboratory and people are the mice, but it does not follow that all writers are misanthropes. Austen became a writer because people fascinated her, warts and all. I became a writer so I could stay home alone. There's a difference.

Many suggested Greta Garbo but I never seriously considered her despite such promising statements as, "For a Swede it is just as natural to be alone as it is for an American to get together." Garbo was more "world-weary" than misanthropic and it's just as well; had she been a misanthrope she would have been an exceedingly frustrated one. Her intense desire to be alone paradoxically required her to cultivate legions of people: the rich whose chateaux and hunting lodges she borrowed to find privacy and solitude; and the entourage of sycophantic fixers who made reservations, handled customs, ordered lunch, and shoved her into taxis so she would not have to deal with people.

Two statements by Garbo convince me that she does not belong in this book. Of swashbuckling Douglas Fairbanks she said, "He makes me feel tired," and in *Grand Hotel* she delivered with striking conviction her famous line, "I have never been so tired in my life." Being a misanthrope would have been too much trouble for this listless, phlegmatic woman. The necessary savage indignation would have demanded too much energy and left her even more exhausted than she already was.

I mention W.C. Fields briefly, but I have left out Oscar Levant, Alan King, Andy Rooney, *et al.* They are not misanthropes but pseudocurmudgeons whose function is to give Americans someone we hate to love, but love anyway. These cute grouches also give real misanthropes a bad name, especially when they turn up on Jerry Lewis's telethons. After all, if you can't hate children, whom can you hate?

I am unable to detect anything as simple as misanthropy in the great monsters of history. Some were insane, like Caligula and Ivan the Terrible. Others, like Hitler, Mussolini, and Stalin, exuded a certain heavy-handed bonhomie (Saddam Hussein appears to belong in this category) that suggests normal conviviality, or at least a willingness to give it a try.

As leaders of great masses of people, monsters must be able to use their personalities to mesmerize their followers and forge primal bonds with them by becoming father figures. Whatever this gift is called—heart, the common touch, public relations— no misanthrope could hold such a pose for more than five minutes, and then only on a good day.

Many monsters, like Adolf Eichmann and his French Revolutionary counterpart, the Jacobin prosecutor Fouquier-Tinville, were also solid middle-class citizens given to civic joinerism, good neighborliness, and exemplary behavior toward friends and family. Hannah Arendt attributed this conundrum to "the banality of evil," but Talleyrand came closer to the mark when he said: "A married man will do anything for money."

Finally, I have eliminated "affectless" psychopaths. Misanthropes were sensitive back when sensitive wasn't cool; to us, life is a Chinese water torture and every drop is a tidal wave. This is not to say, of course, that we aren't psychopathic in our own fashion, but we don't commit crimes because we know that prison life is communal. (If ever you meet someone who cannot understand why solitary confinement is considered punishment, you have met a misanthrope.)

All of the misanthropes I discuss in this book portend or illuminate some contemporary American problem. For this reason, Jonathan Swift, perhaps the most famous misanthrope of all time, makes only a passing appearance. If we discount the effect on his temperament of Menière's disease, which is still being debated and can never be known, the chief cause of Swift's misanthropy seems to have been disgust at the many second-rate people he was forced to deal with in his clerical career. Devious peers and their double-crossing sycophants controlled the church livings and deaneries Swift sought to obtain. His story is a miasma of petty intrigues that, while universal in some respects, offers no striking analogy to American life and is, in my opinion, boring: if you have plowed through one Swiftian fight you have plowed through them all.

I have left out H.L. Mencken for similar reasons. So much has been written about him, especially since the publication of his controversial diary last year, that his misanthropy, while indisputable, has become a cliché. I have chosen instead to include a chapter on his forerunner and idol, Ambrose Bierce, about whom not nearly enough has been written.

I had planned to include Mark Twain and Ring Lardner because both have been called misanthropes by many critics. In Twain's case the assessment is based on the emergence, toward the end of his life, of a "dark side" in his writing. I got tired of reading about this late-blooming "dark side" because misanthropes are born, not made. If Twain's outlook grew bleak in his last decade it was because he was hit by family tragedies—and because it was his last decade. "The Man That Corrupted Hadleyburg" (1899) paints human nature as thoroughly rotten, but it is the normal bitter wisdom of old age, not misanthropy, that speaks to us. America expects old people to exit cute, but some old people refuse to exit cute and Mark Twain was one of them.

He has also been taken too literally, as in his essay "The Damned Human Race," about Man's greatest defect, which he says is "permanent, indestructible, and ineradicable":

I find this Defect to be the *Moral Sense*. He is the only animal that has it. It is the secret of his degradation. It is the quality *which enables him to do wrong*. It has no other office. It is incapable of performing any other function. It could never have been intended to perform any other. Without it, man could do no wrong. He would rise at once to the level of the Higher Animals. Since the Moral Sense has but one office, the one capacity—to enable man to do wrong—it is plainly without value to him.

I read this not as misanthropy but as an intentionally sophistic jeu d'esprit—the moral sense as the clitoris of the human spirit—that rings with the same love of exaggeration that infused his joyous early works.

In his 1929 critique in *The Nation,* Clifton Fadiman accused Ring Lardner of a "perfectly clear simon-pure, deliberate misanthropy." Why? Because his characters are "mental sadists, four-flushers, intolerable gossipers, meal-ticket females, interfering morons, brainless flirts, liars, brutes, spiteful snobs, vulgar climbers, dishonest jockeys, selfish children, dipsomaniacal chorus girls, senile chatterers, idiotically complacent husbands, mean arrivistes, drunks, snoopers, poseurs, and bridge players."

Anyone who would end a list like that with bridge players betrays a certain desperation, and the use of *dipsomaniacal* for *drunken* is cause for deep suspicion, which I promptly developed. It deepened still more when I came across a 1932 assessment by Ludwig Lewisohn, who found "icy hatred and contempt" in Lardner's "bitter and brutal" stories.

I read some of these bitter and brutal stories but their misanthropy eluded me. What did Lardner do to the Lit Crits to make them so mad? The first hint comes in Lewisohn's remark about the ease with which Lardner continued "to sell his merciless tales to the periodicals that cater to the very fools and rogues whom he castigates." The cat comes completely out of the bag with Harry Salpeter's charge in *The Bookman:* "[Lardner] had too many high-priced magazine fish to fry to worry about his place in the pantheon of American literature."

In other words, Lardner remained popular with readers of *The*

Saturday Evening Post after the literati, closet misanthropes without peer, had deigned to discover him.

The Lit Crits were discovering "tragic visions" right and left during the twenties and thirties—Melville was their chief victim—so I took the misanthropy charges against Lardner with a grain of salt. To me, he was an O. Henry in a bad mood or a Lewis Grizzard liberated from good ole boyitis, but not a "simon-pure" misanthrope. Besides, in the course of my research I came across that Fadiman quotation so many times—writers hand down quotations like family silver—that I decided Lardner deserved a break whether he was a misanthrope or not.

Like any other personality trait, misanthropy is a matter of degree. Taken in the literal sense, the obvious problem is one of logistics: hating the entire human race is hard to do—though a few have done it and I will discuss these heroes in subsequent chapters.

In the figurative sense, however, misanthropy is a realistic attitude toward human nature that falls short of the incontinent emotional dependency expressed by Barbra Streisand's anthem to insecurity, "Peepul who need peepul are the luckiest peepul in the world." Considered in this context, an examination of misanthropy has value for Americans who do not necessarily hate everybody, but are tired of compulsory gregariousness, fevered friendliness, we-never-close compassion, goo-goo humanitarianism, sensitivity that never sleeps, and politicians paralyzed by a hunger to be loved.

With the second sense in mind, I have written this book to try and cut through some of the confusion and win one for the Sonofabitch.

A NATION OF
FRIENDLY
MISANTHROPES

When millions of people will go anywhere, bear any burden, and pay any cover price to "feel good about myself," you know that the unconquerable worm is doing his thing in the Republic of Nice.

Niceness as practiced by Americans is a festival of misanthropy denied. We are so afraid of the hostility within us that confrontations barely get started before somebody pops up and announces, "The healing has begun." Fear of getting mad is so widespread that nobody says *mad* anymore. The word is *angry*; somehow it sounds less mad than *mad*.

Initially the word of choice among cheese-bound white winos in the informed 'n' concerned class, the A-word has been so thoroughly drummed into our heads by the media that now it has trickled down to looters. During last spring's riots in Washington's Mount Pleasant district, a participant told the *Washington Post:* "We're angry 'cause of being hassled."

9

FLORENCE KING

To make sure nobody gets *angry* we pre-soften each other constantly in ways that are becoming more and more bizarre. Recently I sent away to a Danish import house for a table that arrived unassembled. I didn't have too much trouble putting it together—it was a five-goddamnit job—but what got me worked up was the packing label: *"Warning! This box contains confusing instructions from Denmark. Please use our friendly instructions packed outside this box."*

Friendly has become a synonym for *clear* and *concise* because clarity and concision are cool qualities. It began with "user-friendly" computers to make cold technology warm, and now nearly every inanimate gismo we use is touted as friendly.

The user-friendly virus has even spread to book reviews, as I discovered recently when I compared the published version of one of mine with the version I wrote.

The fun of writing is in the rewriting. I like to prune every unnecessary word from a piece, to polish and sharpen sentences and arrange them in seamless sequence so that the reader's eye travels effortlessly from left to right in unbroken rhythm as if set on optical cruise control. This is called "tightening"—what Evelyn Waugh was referring to when he wrote in the preface to one of his novels: "If the author had been less industrious, this book would be twice as long."

My review as originally written was as tight as a drum, but when it came out it was loaded up with attributions added by an editorial hand: "according to the author . . . says the author . . . writes the author . . . the author states . . . the author avers . . . in the opinion of the author." All of these grace notes were unnecessary—whom else would I be quoting except the author of the book under review? I had made clear who was speaking with lead-in sentences and colons, but some nervous editor, afraid that *somebody, somewhere,* would misunderstand *something* and get *angry,* had turned my tight copy into an arhythmic sprawl.

The Republic of Nice is embarked on a campaign of no-holds-barred soothing. The entertainment world's time-honored rule, "Always leave 'em laughing," has given way to "Always leave 'em secure." The last segment on news shows now is likely to feature individuals who do strange things for muzzy reasons. A man stands on a street corner every morning and evening during rush hour to wave at passing motorists. A woman in a state that renews driver licenses on the driver's date of birth stands outside the motor vehicles office singing "Happy Birthday" to everyone who goes in. A man cuts the trees on a mountain slope into the shape of a heart that can be seen from miles away so that weary travelers can "take heart": Christ of the Andes meets Burma-Shave.

Asked by the interviewer why he does what he does, the subject shrugs, smiles indulgently at the self-evident question and replies, "I love people." This response has become the designated driver of American attitudes. The psychological test question, *Would you rather work with people or alone?* now ranks with *Own* versus *Rent* on a credit application as an instrument for separating the wheat from the chaff.

The jumpy, black-and-white commercial featuring a tormented soul wringing his hands because his long-distance phone system has ruined his life is usually a prelude to the "Family Of . . ." solution. Americans work for a Family Of, are insured by a Family Of, get their mufflers and brake jobs from a Family Of, buy and sell homes through a Family Of, get moved cross-country by a Family Of. Buy something from a mail-order house and you will become a member of the Damark Family; return it and you will become a member of the UPS Family. What all these firms really are selling is the per-

11

fect security of High Middle Ages feudalism, with the CEO as lord of the manor.

Love never shouts, so the new non-jarring commercials feature dulcet voice-overs. Did you know that no dolphins were harmed to bring you Star-Kist Tuna? A hushed female voice-over informs us that except for a tendency to get caught in tuna nets, the creatures are just like thee and me: "Dolphins talk to each other, and as they get more excited they talk faster and at a higher rate. They have friends among dolphins of the same age, they have one baby at a time, mothers babysit for each other, and the bond between a mother and her young lasts for years."

Star-Kist should get an excited dolphin to do this commercial because the woman's voice is so gentle, soft and low that we can hardly understand it. These whispery (raspy when the voice-over is male) tones are all over the tube these days. At first I thought they were intended to simulate the hissing voice of Satan tempting us to buy, but I have changed my mind. I now think they are the latest thing in Make Nice, the aural equivalent of the linked-arms march after race riots, carefully crafted to sound "unthreatening."

In the Republic of Nice, the soft-spoken are King. Television anchors, who must somehow project an air of unthreatening authority, are lately solving this conundrum by swallowing the end of their sentences to avoid a sharp, strident delivery. The worst offender is Peter Jennings. His voice drops and disappears into a prissy smirk and a little nod reminiscent of the unassertive women Colette Dowling describes in *The Cinderella Complex,* whose speech patterns she calls the "Diffident Declarative."

The Republic of Nice has a Rumpelstiltsken Complex. Living in dread of exploding in foot-stamping, purple-faced rage like the foul-tempered gnome in the fairy tale, we have devised comparable precautions.

Plugging up safety valves is our favorite way of keeping every-body calm. In her horrified appraisal of my last book, *Lump It or Leave It,* Martha Peters of the *El Paso Times* insists that "satire is only funny when it is neither embittered nor mean." That would be news to several people in the present book, but Walter B. Schwab of Providence puts Ambrose Bierce and Ana-tole France in their place in his May 14, 1990, letter to *Time:* "Disparaging humor is verbal abuse and can be as damaging as the physical kind, if not more so. It destroys self-esteem."

A Nashville obstetrics ward became a brooding ground of self-esteem when a couple sued the hospital for $4 million on learning that the nurses had nicknamed their baby daughter "Smurfette" because she was born blue from blue dye injected into her mother's womb during a prenatal test.

"Painful though these events have been, we have all learned a great deal about how sensitive and fragile our society is, how deeply people and groups can be hurt if great care is not taken in conducting public discourse."

No, that has nothing to do with Smurfette. That's CBS presi-dent David Burke after suspending Andy Rooney for allegedly making cracks about people of another color, but it fits any self-esteem emergency. It also fits on a Miranda-sized card so that the five remaining spontaneous citizens of the Republic of Nice can carry it around in their wallets in case they slip up and say what they think.

Code words are pretty packages full of friendly instructions in which we wrap our real meanings. Some, like *inner city,* have been around for years, but the one that is all the rage lately is *dialogue.*

I caused a dialogue here in Fredericksburg, Virginia when I wrote an op-ed for our local paper, the *Free Lance-Star.*

Fredericksburg, which lies sixty miles south of the Nation's

Capital, is turning into a suburb of it. Federal government employees who can no longer tolerate or afford the original suburban Virginia counties of Arlington and Fairfax are moving here in droves to find solace in our relaxed "lifestyle," which is being steadily destroyed by their increasing presence.

I got tired of hearing the locals castigate the come-heres in private, so I decided to do what the Republic of Nice calls "explore" the problem and "address" the issue. I called the newcomers Yankee yuppies, said they were either rootless or from Illinois, accused them of eating cheese that looks like a unicorn's miscarriage, and recommended that the counties of Arlington and Fairfax secede from Virginia and form a separate state so the rest of us will not have to pay for their roads.

I gave my op-ed to the editor of the paper, who passed it on to his assistant and then left for a fact-finding mission to China. The night the piece was published, our little corner of the Republic of Nice went up in smoke. I received congratulatory phone calls from people with Southern accents, who identified themselves; and violently abusive anonymous phone calls, including two death threats, from people with Northern accents. The next day I bought my first answering machine and the phone calls changed from spoken words to hard breathing and Bronx cheers.

The paper received more letters than it had ever gotten on any subject. The newcomers called me a fascist, an elitist, a "Fredneck," and that favorite of book reviewers, *mean-spirited*. The Southerners who wrote in support of me called the newcomers "carpetbaggers," blamed them for traffic jams and tax hikes levied "to pay for schools for their doped-up kids," and suggested that the Rappahannock River be turned into a moat to deflect Northern migration.

The uproar attracted the attention of Washington's NBC-TV, who sent a team down to cover it. After a few picturesque shots

of Fredericksburg, they interviewed the newspaper editor looking pale and drawn behind his letter-piled desk, followed by an
interview with me in which I expanded my original secession
idea.

"The Northern Virginia counties and the suburban Maryland
counties should hook up together and form a separate state with
Washington as its capital," I said. "Then they can make one big
pothole out of the place."

The television coverage fanned the flames all over again. More
letters-to-the-editor poured in, but this time I garnered a fervent
supporter from the Yankee-yuppie contingent. A Fredericksburg
newcomer originally from Wisconsin, he picked up on my anti-
Illinois crack and wrote in to say that he didn't like Illinois
people either because they vacationed in Wisconsin and clogged
up the roads. This drew a letter from an Illinois native who said
that Wisconsin didn't have any roads worth driving on. By the
time a Minnesotan got in it, they had forgotten all about me and
were fighting with each other.

The paper devoted the lead editorial to my brouhaha, announcing in tones of solemn approbation: "A dialogue has
begun."

More recently, the *Free Lance-Star* reported on a speech delivered at Fredericksburg's Mary Washington College by a member
of the Nation of Islam. It was the usual Farrakhan farrago: up
with Hitler, down with Jews and other whites, plus a locally
tailored insult to George Washington's mother, for whom the
college is named. As a final fillip, he tossed in a pan review of
Driving Miss Daisy for its portrayal of affection between the
races.

The speech triggered hysteria on campus; so many students
were weeping and raging and getting into disputes that profes-
sors had to use class time for "tension-defusing" discussions of

15

racial issues. The letters-to-the-editor column divided along black-white lines and a town-gown split emerged, but how did the college administration describe it all?

The banner headline read: MUSLIM SPEECH CREDITED FOR SPURRING DIALOGUE.

Another way the Republic of Nice puts the lid on its Rumpelstiltsken Complex is through "stress management," a phrase so suggestive of gritted teeth that you can almost hear the scrunch.

To keep Americans from dying in the prime of nice, the stress industry has abandoned medicine's earlier claim that letting off steam is good for you. Now we read: TRUST HELPS HEARTS. BLOWING YOUR TOP COULD BE HAZARDOUS TO YOUR HEALTH, TWO STUDIES INDICATE.

One of these "wellness" studies took place at Duke University, the house that tobacco built, and involved 118 male lawyers who scored "hostile" on a personality test. The testees were prone to "antagonistic interaction," and were described as "rude, abrasive, surly, critical, uncooperative, condescending, and disagreeable"—the law firm of choice for litigious Americans.

Among the researchers on this study was Dr. Redford B. Williams, Jr., author of *The Trusting Heart,* who warns: "Having anger is bad for you, whether you express it or not. But we found that people who said they made a point of letting other people know they were angry had higher death rates."

The best way to bottle up anger is to turn men into women. After years of consensus seeking, reaching out, coming together, building bridges, linking arms, and tying yellow ribbons, the feminization of America is now complete. American men have been turned into their own secret police, under orders to kick down their own doors in the middle of the night and arrest themselves for "insensitivity."

A foremost beau ideal of the New Man is columnist Richard

Cohen, the *Washington Post*'s resident oh-dear, who is such a world-class bundle of sensitivity that if he had been on the *Titanic* he would have apologized for damage to the iceberg. Male soul-searching is in and Cohen is its undisputed champ, having searched his own so often that he has become Butterfly Dundee, the man every woman would least like to have with her if she met a mugger.

The feminization of America is so pervasive that it has even changed the way men talk, not just their tones but the whole thrust of their conversations. Persuaded that normal masculine directness and unequivocality might make people *angry,* today's men have adopted the age-old feminine stratagem of hurt feelings and the newer feminist technique of politicized nagging to get their points across. Our national discourse now is conducted in a baritone tsk-tsking tut-tuttery, as when a snippy Dan Rather demanded of his man in Alaska: "Did Hazelwood ever apologize for the Valdez oil spill?"

It has spread beyond the press and academia to such bastions of testosterone as the National Rifle Association, from whom I received an unbelievable computer-written letter signed by Wayne LaPierre.

Since the NRA membership is overwhelmingly male, it would be interesting to know the reaction of the thousands of brawny hunters who must have received one just like it. It is by turns a billet doux, a Jewish mother's kvetch, and a haunting reminder of those sweetly threatening Girls Dorm Council reports about what happens to people who leave starch on the bottom of the iron. It is four pages long thanks to the user-friendly practice of ridiculously short paragraphs; nonetheless, I must quote it in full to render its indescribable flavor, and to prove my contention that Alexander Portnoy never had to put up with anything like it.

FLORENCE KING

Mind you, I have never met or spoken to Wayne LaPierre, but this is what he said:

Dear Florence:

I need to know if we're still friends.

I know you normally receive legislative alerts from me every so often and, after a while, they all start to look alike.

But this is a personal letter from me to you.

You see, I have realized that every person reaches a point where they must take stock of all they have done.

You begin to take inventory of what your life has represented. You reflect on your motives, goals, ambitions and accomplishments.

In the end, you realize that the best gauge of a successful life comes from the friendships you have made.

That's why I am contacting you personally. To see if our friendship, forged in 1989, to fight the anti-gun and anti-hunting crowd is still as strong as ever.

To tell you the truth, this year has been one of the most trying for me and the NRA.

I simply haven't stopped for a minute trying to put out the brushfires Handgun Control, Inc. has started in Congress and in almost all 50 state legislatures.

I'm constantly in and out of state capitals and hearings and continually cross-examined on national and local news programs. Sometimes just for a few minutes, sometimes for hours.

When the big votes come up in Congress, the demands never stop.

But this is the course I have chosen. Because I think it is crucial that we convey our message about our Constitutional right to keep and bear arms.

18

By taking this path, the times become very trying and exhausting. And time away from work becomes virtually non-existent.

But I'm committed to my job because I know I speak for many Americans who will not allow their gun rights to be abolished. And your voice and mine must be heard!

At this point, I think of you.

Do you approve of what I'm saying and what I'm doing?

Every time someone puts a microphone in my face, I think for a minute how you feel . . . how you might respond. . . .

What worries me the most is that I haven't heard from you in quite a while. I personally checked and found no contribution from you since 1989. Only through your contributions can NRA-ILA continue it's [sic] work. And unless I'm wrong, we haven't even gotten a personal letter of encouragement from you during that time.

Which leads me to ask—do I still speak for you?

I am proud of the fact that when the battle was heating up in 1989, you took the time and stood by me. You added your efforts to mine to help protect our gun rights.

With all that's gone on in the past year, I cannot deny that I miss your ongoing support. I do. Our program desperately needs your continued help. And your NRA dues cannot be used to fight the battles NRA-ILA faces.

But more importantly, I miss hearing from you.

The National Rifle Association is built on our standing together.

That's why it is so important to me that this friendship not just become another fond recollection of the past. Or a friendship that is just forgotten.

I certainly understand that budgets get tight and not everyone can make a gift every year. I know I've called on you to write your

Congressman and Senators and you might have done it and I just don't know about it. And if you have, I want to say thank you.

I've asked you to do so much.

But I'd like you to take just a minute to hand write a note or use the enclosed card to check off that I'm on target . . . that I'm still on track . . . that when I'm interviewed by the press or representing gun owners in the U.S. Congress, I'm still speaking for you.

So, please drop me a line and let me know that we are still fighting for the same goals. And, if you are able to include your special $50 for the cause we have all fought so hard for, that would let me know how much you still care.

This is important. Very important. I'm not just writing to ask you to send a contribution. I'm writing because I want to keep our friendship strong.

We've seen too much as friends to just lose each other in the shuffle of the battles we must fight.

And by hearing from you today, I will be able to continue to produce our hard-hitting ads to fight the anti-gunners and anti-hunters in the media, the Congress, and the 50 state legislatures.

Each time I must walk onto a platform to speak or face a badgering circle of microphones, I will know that the strength of what I say is much more than just words, it's more than my voice, it's yours as well.

Unless you're there, standing with me, the cause we share is greatly diminished.

I will be looking forward to your response.

All my best,
Wayne

How many NRA fund raisers does it take to change a light-bulb? None: "Don't worry about me, go out and enjoy yourself, I'll just sit here alone in the dark."

The feminization of America was supposed to banish Rumpel-stiltsken permanently but it is likely to have the opposite effect. Nothing is more infuriating than female stratagems. With her silken weaponry of ambivalence, circularity, and freighted silences, woman burrows into her adversary's very soul—sideways, like a tick crossed with a mole crossed with a crab. This modus operandi has filled everything from the French Foreign Legion to battered-wife shelters, yet America thinks it will keep the peace.

Our feminized niceness has mired us in a soft, sickly, helpless tolerance of everything. America is the girl who can't say no, the town pump who lets anybody have a go at her. We are a single-parent country with no father to cut through the molasses and point out, for example, the inconsistency of embracing warm and compassionate "values" while condemning cold and detached "value judgments."

This popular mental somersault was evident in the case of Jim Dickson, the blind yachtsman who conceived the foolhardy idea of sailing the Atlantic alone. In our motherish rush to give the testy Dickson his way, we forgot all about the sighted sailors whose crafts he could have rammed, and the Coast Guardsmen who might have had to die for the sake of niceness at any price. The only person who dared say *no* to Dickson was William F. Buckley, Jr., whose warnings brought down the wrath of the Republic of Nice on his head, complete with plummy epithets such as "paternalistic sightist."

Our feminized niceness keeps us from solving our most pressing problems, such as crime. In our treatment of criminals we are like the mother-heart in the fable about the boy whose sweetheart commands him to cut out his mother's heart and bring it to her as proof of his devotion. He obediently cuts out the heart, but as he hurries to his sweetheart's house with it, he stumbles

21

and falls, whereupon the heart speaks: "Are you hurt, my son?"

The only way to handle the criminal is to whip his ass till his nose bleeds buttermilk, but the few unequivocal souls who are willing to unleash such curative measures shun politics because they know they would never even get nominated, much less elected. Captive of female priorities, America instinctively shrinks from the only kind of personality capable of solving the problems we constantly deplore. From the White House down, we vote only for candidates whose eyes plead "Like me."

Bruno Bettleheim said, "The deepest of all human anxieties is to be at the mercy of one's own impulses." Instead of "humanizing" men, it would have been far better if women had copied men's stoic *virtus*. A nation of self-controlled people is less likely to blow than one giving off beta-consciousness waves. The hatreds we are trying to tamp down and deny have a much better chance of coming to the surface when people are "in touch with their feelings." And if they do, they will be all the more violent from having been so long subjected to the feminized tactics of the Republic of Nice.

The suspicion that David Souter might be a misanthropic hermit sent the Republic of Nice into a tailspin when the fifty-year-old bachelor was nominated to the Supreme Court.

"Judge Souter is our Rorschach test," wrote *Washington Times* columnist Suzanne Fields, "telling us more about ourselves than about him." He certainly did. The vaunted independence that Americans cherish consists of two things: the single-issue pressure group and the automobile. We boast about our rugged individualism, yet when an avatar of it draws near to a position of power, we go crazy.

Women's groups demanded reassurance that Souter would

"empathize" with women's issues. Presumably they meant "sympathize," though with feminists you never know.

Elizabeth Chittick, honorary president of the National Woman's Party, proclaimed: "The fact that he's 50 and not married tells me he's anti-women."

Alan Dershowitz seemed to hint at something really nasty: "I mean, this is a 50-year-old bachelor who lives with sheep in Weare, N.H., out of this world."

Time called him "An 18th-Century Man," forgetting that the Founding Fathers were too, and warned: "The more serious question about Souter's ascetic ways is whether a man who seems to prefer books to people can empathize [there it is again] with and understand the problems of ordinary people."

Kenneth Adelman gave Souter advice on how to handle the hearings: "You have to show yourself in a sincere manner. Don't be afraid to show emotions about the passionate issues of the day. Show concern, show care, show feeling."

Finally, somebody dredged up a Souter date from the early sixties, Ellanor Stengel Fink, who did her best to reassure the citizens of America "Я" Us.

"What doesn't come across in the accounts I've read is what a warm, friendly guy he can be," she rhapsodized. "He comes across as a steely intellectual. All head and no heart. He is a very bright person and very interesting, but he's not all brain. He's a friendly, warm person and extremely considerate." And not only that, his parents were "very warm, friendly lovely people. A traditional, close family."

That does not necessarily guarantee a brilliant Supreme Court career, and it certainly doesn't guarantee a long one. To paraphrase Nietzsche, relatives have probably killed more people than the cholera—a forbidden view in the Republic of Nice but one that rears its subliminal head in the low-fat margarine commercial: *"Love your family twenty-five percent less!"*

Souter is no longer in a position to reveal to the Republic of Nice the title of the steely intellectual's favorite holiday ditty, but there is nothing stopping me. It's called "I'll Be Lone for Christmas, You Can Bet Your Ass."

I have no doubt that many people fully expected Souter's isolated cellar to yield up a dozen or so female corpses murdered by him over the years. And why not? Every newspaper reader in the Republic of Nice knows what murderers are like: SLAYING SUSPECT DESCRIBED AS LONER.

According to the suspect's neighbors, he "kept himself to himself" and "had trouble at work." But the victim? Listen to his neighbors: "Everybody loved him, he got along with everybody. He didn't have an enemy in the world. He was such a happy person, always helping people. I remember he always said a stranger is a friend you haven't met yet. He would give you the shirt off his back. One day a homeless person came to the door and asked him for a drink of water, and he invited him in for a meal. He was always smiling, I never saw him frown, no, not once. Our kids were crazy about him."

To suggest that this hot, wet paragon might have had a fatal flaw, and that it might have had something to do with America's blackout of the maxim, "Everybody's friend is everybody's fool," is not permitted. Nonetheless, it is a truth universally unacknowledged that loners go happily through life, keeping themselves to themselves and having trouble at work until they die in their beds at ninety-six. "Hell," said Jean-Paul Sartre, "is other people."

A NATION OF
MISANTHROPIC FRIENDS

Across the border from the Republic of Nice is the Republic of Mean, home of the closet misanthrope, where feeling better about oneself takes the form of a petty, ad hoc, peekaboo loathing of humankind that no real misanthrope would have time for.

How about some proportional misanthropy? It goes well with proportional representation. George Bush in Omaha: "It's good to be away from Washington and out here with the *real* people." Rosalynn Carter's press secretary: "She's in touch with the *real* people." The National Beef Council: "Beef! Real food for *real* people!" Take your pick and hate the rest.

Not since Pompeiians yelled "Run!" have so many people surged in the same direction at once as the great hordes presently going to law school. Asked why they want to be lawyers, these fledgling Perrys and Portias recite various conventional reasons, including, incredibly, "I want to help people." The real reason, never voiced, is: "I want to learn how to be mean."

Egged on by the compassion-impaired, many of the handicapped have turned into ogres who relish every opportunity to
hurl epithets at anyone who says "confined" to a wheelchair, or
who does *not* say "differently abled" instead of handicapped.
Somerset Maugham anticipated these closet misanthropes. "It is
not true," he wrote, "that suffering ennobles the character; happiness does that sometimes, but suffering, for the most part,
makes men petty and vindictive."

Sick jokes have been officially outlawed by the compassion-
impaired but substitutes can be found in perfectly respectable
newspapers. Masquerading under the guise of human interest
and bearing innocent headings such as "Around the Nation" or
"News in Brief" are little squibs about the activities of cretins
that get clipped and enclosed in letters exchanged by people who
have not yet been rendered brain-dead by the machinations of
the sensitivity industry.

I file mine in a folder marked *Idiocy: General* to save for my
agent. Among those I have sent him is the one about a man who
axed his mother-in-law to death in a dark garage in the belief that
she was a giant raccoon. Another, which I reheadlined MURDER
AT SECOND BASE, was about two Little League mothers who got
into an infield shoot-out that left one dead.

My agent sent me one about a man who sued a saloon after a
faulty switch on an adjustable "knock-back" drinking chair
catapulted him through a plate-glass window. I responded with
BABY FOUND ASLEEP IN GETAWAY CAR (the bankrobber's sitter
didn't show up), and UNBURIED CORPSE FOUND ON SOFA (the body
of a woman who had been dead for two years was found on a
sofa, fully clothed, at the home of her daughter, who told police
that she hadn't known what to do with it).

Inevitably, the day came when we sent each other the same
clipping: NEWLYWEDS ELECTROCUTED BY TUBSIDE TV.

"Decade-ism" is an ideal sport for the closet misanthrope who wants to remain securely in the closet. Decades are full of people, so if you hurry up and hate the decade just past, you can hate just about everybody now alive, yet be accused of nothing stronger than a sense of history.

Perpetually irritable intellectuals too liberal to admit how irritable they are tend to have a great sense of history. As soon as a zero turned up at the end of their date stamps last year, pundits in the Land of Hopefully and Glory took thoughtful flying leaps into a literal yesterday, turning op-ed pages into festivals of self-flagellation with misanthropic undertones as they condemned the "Reagan Decade" for its buccaneering greed and administered sound thrashings to everyone who did not spend the eighties in a hair shirt.

Decade-ism gives closet misanthropes of the Republic of Mean a perfect out. No matter how much they berate the decade just past, they can still get credit for being good citizens of the Republic of Nice by announcing that they are looking forward to the kinder 'n' gentler decade coming up.

Our eagerness to get away from each other has made the ubiquitous "Ten Most Livable Cities" article beloved by closet misanthropes.

Americans are desperate to escape crime, pollution, noise, rudeness, and traffic jams—*i.e.,* people. Once they move somewhere new to get away from people, they discover they are hated by people who hate people who are trying to get away from people they hate. This is known to Style editors as: "A Town in Transition, Fighting to Preserve Its Historic [rural, traditional, unique, Norman Rockwell] Character."

The new migrations are proving that the Welcome Wagon is dead. I see the handwriting on the mall, and it's a bumper sticker:

Seattle: Don't Californicate the State of Washington
Oregon: Come See Us But Go Back Home
Atlanta: General Sherman, Where Are You Now That We
Need You?
Fredericksburg: If You Ain't a Rebel, You Ain't Shit

Rainbow misanthropy? It's a mystery to me how anyone can look at the proliferation of support groups and not see them for what they really are: a lunatic quest for birds of a feather by people so sick of our Great Diversity that they unconsciously reject it by joining Tone-Deaf Parents of Left-Handed Anorexic Kleptomaniacs just to be with their own kind.

A leading rainbow misanthrope is Sonny Carson, the black convicted kidnapper who worked in the campaign of New York Mayor David "Gorgeous Mosaic" Dinkins. Accused of being anti-Semitic, Carson replied: "Anti-Semitic? I'm anti-white. Don't limit my anti-ing to just being one little group of people." Spoken like a true misanthrope: Don't think small, I hate everybody.

A movement toward equality of bigotry is leading to misanthropy by accretion. Karen Schwartz of the Gay and Lesbian Alliance Against Defamation (GLAAD) commented on the Andy Rooney flap with the statement: "GLAAD opposes all forms of bigotry and believes that if you scratch a homophobe you'll probably find a racist." By this logic, the scratched racist, if scratched repeatedly, will prove to be anti-Semitic, will prove to be anti-Catholic, will prove to be anti-Slavic, and so on down the list until we achieve raw misanthropy—literally.

A similar accretion is taking shape in the sex war. In the early days of the women's movement, when *misogyny* was on every tongue, some writers, feminists among them, misued *misanthropy* in the belief that it meant hatred of *males.* Misogyny's correct mate is *misandry;* a woman who hates men is a *misandrist.* You can do wonders with a matched set, as Walt Whitman demonstrated when he defined America as the place where "the men hate the women and the women hate the men." If half the population is misogynistic and the other half misandristic, America is thus a misanthropic whole. Misogyny and misandry are simply substitutes for misanthropy among those who are not quite ready to take that giant step for mankind.

The darkling obsessions that feminists develop mark them as closet misanthropes. For the past several years, their leading obsession has been incest. They have gone to the mat with it, but the American media maw demands constant stoking, so they can't get much more mileage out of it. A feminist without an obsession is like Abbott without Costello, so what other age-old perversion is waiting in the wings? Today, incest; tomorrow—what?

We must turn to Mary Daly for a preview of coming attractions. In a May 10, 1989 *New York Times* article about her ongoing struggle to obtain tenure at Boston College, she is quoted as saying that Christianity and all other major faiths, as well as Marxism and Freudianism, are patriarchal forms whose "entire message is necrophilia."

The turning-inward, the retreat into oneself implicit in incest is exceeded only by the ultimate solitude of necrophilia. Feminists who go around looking for either of these perversions have very little love for mankind regardless of how many linked-arms marches and candlelight vigils they participate in.

Involuntary euthanasia is a closet misanthrope's fantasy at the moment but I predict it will catch on. In America no one is evil, things just catch on, helped along by our penchant for inventing words to justify the conclusions we have already reached.

Now that legal abortion has gotten people used to counting in

FLORENCE KING

trimesters, the *when* of euthanasia will be easy to manage. We will acquire a new buzzword, "lifeness." Not death but simply less-than-life. If trimesters are valid measurements at the start, why not "lifenesses" at the end? It's bound to appeal to Americans. Awkward words always do.

Old people know perfectly well that a great deal of closet misanthropy is directed at them. Their fear of hatred is pitiful to behold, but worse are their attempts to deflect it. Every once in a while, newspapers and magazines will contain a letter from a senior citizen in defense of young people, particularly teens. "A boy helped me change my tire. . . . it's good to see the young people enjoying themselves. . . . we often sit on our porch and watch the skateboarders. . . . we always schedule our trips to the supermarket on Friday nights so we can enjoy the camaraderie of cruising night as the youngsters drive around and around the shopping center in leisurely fashion, greeting their friends with jaunty halloos [truly!]."

These letters are sometimes triggered by an article critical of kids, but most of the time they are pathetic non sequiturs triggered by nothing—except perhaps the blithe use of the word "geezer" by closet misanthropes in the media.

Lest anyone think that gerontophobia has been driven out by political correctness, think again. Smith College recently made a not-so-subtle change in the definition of *ageism* in its PC handbook. It now means "oppression of the young and old by young adults and the middle-aged." In America, anyone who shares billing with children ends up leaving the stage, often with the help of a vaudeville hook.

The widespread hatred of television is a form of closet misanthropy of special interest to anyone who grew up in the radio era. We didn't hate radio and blame it for all sorts of ills. We didn't worry about how many hours a day our radios were on, we

30

didn't lie about our radio habits ("I never listen to it"). We didn't claim that radio invaded our privacy, and our newspapers did not contain self-help pieces entitled "Turning Off the Radio Habit."

Today we have Judy Mann in the *Washington Post* on "Turning Off the TV Habit," about her family's cold-turkey withdrawal from the electronic beast.

"I don't miss it at all," she insists in the third paragraph. It's a one-sentence paragraph, set apart and standing alone for greater dramatic emphasis.

She goes on to say, "You realize how stupid the sitcoms are," "It is a terrible time-waster," and "Television is a lot like smoking: You only realize what a rotten habit it is once you've stopped." She also quotes her husband—"He thinks it destroys the mind"—and a Washington-area English teacher: "If TV is like a drug that numbs the mind, excessive viewing amounts to drug abuse."

These vitriolic reactions echo the fashionable complaint that television is "an insult to the intelligence," but intelligence is the handmaiden of cool reason, and something hotter is at work here.

Television rouses our instinctive hatred because it is the only medium of entertainment in which the great do not keep their distance. Theater actors perform on a curtained stage, radio is a disembodied voice, and movies of the thirties and forties presented godlike stars who were figuratively larger than life and made them literally larger than life on giant screens. But the democratic size of the television screen and its permanent presence in our homes have deprived us of personages awesome and mysterious, damaging thereby the psychic dynamo that powers religious faith. In the primitive recesses of our minds, television

FLORENCE KING

personalities are to us what antichrists and heretics were to the Middle Ages.

The most revolting form of closet misanthropy in the Republic of Mean is the "Oprah's Guest" syndrome. Masquerading as compassionate broad-mindedness but really driven by the notion that dignity is elitist, it demands that people strip themselves of all that is seemly and wallow in maudlin sludge.

MARYLAND COUPLE SHARES A GIFT OF LOVE: HER KIDNEY

After the area's first spousal transplant, the couple "crept together through the hospital corridors, both slightly bent with pain," while their teenage children "hung out with them, looking after mom and dad and making home videos of them."

When they left the hospital to go home, the husband wore a teeshirt inscribed: "My wife gave me her heart and all her love. Now she gave me a kidney." He explained: "I was so glad. I had my catheter and my bag of what we call liquid gold. I said, 'Timmie, look at this,' " meaning that the new kidney was working.

Added the *Washington Post* reporter: "The Warners are the kind of people who view obstacles as challenges—the glass half full, not half empty, as Kenneth Warner put it. And they are 'goal-oriented' people, he said. Warner decided he wanted a transplant kidney, and he set Christmas as his personal deadline."

But who would donate it? Said Mrs. Warner: "We woke up on a Saturday morning and I said 'Why can't I give you a kidney?' " And so she did. And left the hospital wearing a teeshirt inscribed: "I gave my husband my heart and all my love. Now I gave him a kidney."

My coffee cup is half empty. While I pour myself a refill, look at this:

It's a Christmas postcard from Congressperson Patricia

Schroeder, who evidently culled my name from the *MS.* subscription list. The picture shows the whole family, including the dog, frolicking in the snow. The message reads: "Santa's back! So are Jim, Pat, Scott, Jamie & Wolfie Schroeder! Jamie is a sophomore at Princeton studying Chinese. Scott works at ABC News in D.C. Jim works at paying bills and Pat works at passing them! Wolfie sleeps! Best Holiday Wishes for a great 1990. Pat & the gang."

The home address is up in the corner, designed to look hastily written by hand instead of photocopied: Schroeder, 1600 Emerson, Denver CO 80218. And of course, *Pat* contains a smiley face in the circle of the *P.*

It is not necessary to like people to respect them. The Warners and Schroeders among us miss a vital point that we of cooler temperaments instinctively understand and unfailingly honor: Familiarity doesn't breed contempt, it *is* contempt.

Hatred of smokers is the leading form of closet misanthropy in the Republic of Mean. Smokists don't hate the sin, they hate the sinner.

The anti-tobacco campaign never would have succeeded so well if the alleged dangers of smoking had remained a problem for smokers alone. We simply would have been allowed to invoke the Right to Die, always a favorite with democratic lovers of mankind, and that would have been that. To put a real damper on smoking and make it stick, the right of others not to die had to be invoked somehow, so "passive smoking" was invented.

The name was a stroke of genius. Just about everybody in America is passive. Passive Americans have been taking it on the chin for years, but the concept of passive smoking offered them a chance to hate in the land of compulsory love, a chance to dish it out for a change with no fear of being called a bigot.

The big, brave Passive Americans responded with a vengeance. They began shouting at smokers in restaurants. They shuddered and grimaced and said "Ugh!" as they waved away the impure air. They put up little signs in their cars and homes. At first they said Thank You for Not Smoking but now they feature a cigarette in a circle slashed with a red diagonal. They even issue conditional invitations—I got one. The woman said, "I'd love to have you to dinner but I don't allow smoking in my home. Do you think you could refrain for a couple of hours?" I said "Go fuck yourself" and she told everybody I was the rudest person she had ever met.

Insisting that there is no difference between tobacco and hard drugs, they equate cigarette smokers with heroin, cocaine, and crack users and call us "addicts." Curiously, however, we are the only ones they are willing to berate publicly. If they really believe all addicts are equal, why don't they walk up to crackheads and mainliners and scream "Ugh! You're disgusting!"

Because they are afraid of getting killed.

Washington Times columnist and smoker Jeremiah O'Leary was the target of two incredibly baleful letters to the editor after he defended the habit. The first one said, "Smoke yourself to death, but please don't smoke me to death," but it was only a foretaste of the second:

Jeremiah O'Leary's March 1 column, "Perilous persuaders . . . tenacious zealots," is a typical statement of a drug addict trying to defend his vice.

To a cigarette smoker, all the world is an ashtray. A person who would never throw a candy wrapper or soda can will drop a lit cigarette without a thought.

Mr. O'Leary is mistaken that non-smokers are concerned about the damage smokers are inflicting on themselves. What arrogance! We care about living in a pleasant environment without the stench of tobacco smoke or the litter of smoker's trash.

If Mr. O'Leary wants to kill himself, that is his choice. I ask only that he do so without imposing his drug or discarded filth on me. *It would be nice if he would die in such a way that would not increase my health insurance rates.* [my italics]

The expendability of smokers has also aroused the closet misanthropy of the federal government. I was taking my first drag of the morning when I opened the *Washington Post* and found myself staring at this headline: NOT SMOKING COULD BE HAZARDOUS TO PENSION SYSTEM. MEDICARE, SOCIAL SECURITY MAY BE PINCHED IF ANTI-TOBACCO CAMPAIGN SUCCEEDS, REPORT SAYS.

The article explained that since smokers die younger than non-smokers, the Social Security we don't live to collect is put to good use, because we subsidize the pensions of our fellow citizens like a good American should. However, this convenient arrangement could end, for if too many smokers heed the Surgeon General's warnings and stop smoking, they will live too long and break the budget.

That, of course, is not how the government economists phrased it. They said:

The implications of our results are that smokers "save" the Social Security system hundreds of billions of dollars. Certainly this does not mean that decreased smoking would not be socially beneficial. In fact, it is probably one of the most cost-effective ways of increasing average longevity. It does indicate, however, that if people alter their behavior in a manner which extends life

expectancy, then this must be recognized by our national retirement program.

At this point the reporter steps in with the soothing reminder
that "the war on tobacco is more appropriately cast as a public
health crusade than as an attempt to save money." But then we
hear from Health Policy Center economist Gio Gori, who said:
"Prevention of disease is obviously something we should strive
for. But it's not going to be cheap. We will have to pay for those
who survive."

Something darkling crawls out of that last sentence. The whole
article has a die-damn-you undertow that makes an honest misanthrope wonder if perhaps a cure for cancer was discovered
years ago, but due to cost-effective considerations. . . .

But honest misanthropes are at a premium that no amount of
Raleigh coupons can buy. Instead we have tin-pot Torquemadas
like Ahron Leichtman, president of Citizens Against Tobacco
Smoke, who announced after the airline smoking ban: "CATS
will next launch its smoke-free airports project, which is the
second phase of our smoke-free skies campaign."

Rep. Richard J. Durbin promised the next target will be "other
forms of public transportation such as Amtrak, the intercity bus
system and commuter lines that receive federal funding." His
colleague, Sen. Frank Lautenberg, confessed, "We *are* gloating
a little bit," and Fran du Melle of the Coalition on Smoking OR
Health, gave an ominous hint of things to come when she her-
alded the airline ban as "only one encouraging step on the road
to a smoke-free society."

These remarks manifest a sly, cowardly form of misanthropy
that the Germans call *Schadenfreude:* pleasure in the unhappi-
ness of others. It has always been the chief subconscious motiva-

tion of puritans, but the smokists harbor several other sub-conscious motivations that are even more loathsome.

Study their agitprop and you will find the same theme of pitiless revulsion running through nearly all of their public-service ads. One of the earliest showed Brooke Shields toweling her wet hair and saying disgustedly, "I hate it when somebody smokes after I've just washed my hair. Yuk!" Another pro-claimed, "Kissing a smoker is like licking an ashtray." The latest, a California radio spot, asks: "Why sell cigarettes? Why not just sell phlegm and cut out the middle man?"

Fear of being physically disgusting and smelling bad is the insecure American's worst nightmare, which is why bath-soap commercials never include the flow-restricting shower nozzles that environmentalists push in *their* public-service ads. The showering American always uses oceans of hot water to get "ZESTfully clean" in a sudsy deluge.

Next comes a deodorant commercial. "Raise your hand, raise your hand, raise your hand if you're SURE!" During this jingle we see an ecstatically happy assortment of people from all walks of life and representing every conceivable national origin, all obediently raising their hands, until the ad climaxes with a shot of the Statue of Liberty raising hers.

The Statue of Liberty is a symbol of immigration, the first aspect of American life that the huddled masses experienced. The second was being called a "dirty little" something-or-other as soon as they got off the boat. Deodorant companies see the wisdom in reminding the immigrants' descendants of the dirty-little period in their family histories. You can sell a lot of deodor-ant this way. Ethnics get the point directly; Wasps get it by default in the subliminal reminder that, historically speaking, there is no such thing as a dirty little Wasp.

Smokers are the new greenhorns in the land of sweetness and

health, scapegoats for a quintessentially American need, rooted in our fabled Great Diversity, to identify and punish the undesirables among us. Ethnic tobacco haters can get even for past slurs on their fastidiousness by refusing to inhale around dirty little smokers, and Wasp tobacco haters can savor once again the joy of being "real" Americans by hurling with impunity the same dirty little insults that their ancestors hurled with impunity.

The tobacco pogrom serves additionally as the basis for a class war in a nation afraid to mention the word *class* aloud. Hating smokers is an excellent way to hate the white workingclass without going on record as hating the white workingclass.

The anti-smoking campaign has enjoyed thumping success among the "data-receptive," a lovely euphemism describing the privilege of spending four years taking notes on the jawboning of asses. The ubiquitous statistic that college graduates are two-and-a-half times as likely to be non-smokers as those who never went beyond high school is balm to the data-receptive, many of whom are only a generation or two removed from the lunchbucket that smokers represent. Haunted by a fear of falling back down the ladder, and half-believing that they deserve to, they soothe their anxiety by kicking a smoker as the proverbial henpecked husband soothed his by kicking the dog.

The earnest shock that greeted the RJR Reynolds "Uptown" marketing scheme aimed at blacks cramped the vituperative style of the data-receptive. Looking down on blacks as smokers might be interpreted as looking down on blacks as blacks, so they settled for aping the compassionate concern they picked up from the media.

They got their misanthropy-receptive bona fides back when the same company announced plans to target "Dakota" cigarettes at a fearsome group called "virile females."

When I first saw the headline I thought surely they meant me:

what other woman writer is sent off to a book-and-author luncheon with the warning, "Watch your language and don't wear your Baltimore Orioles warm-up jacket"? But no. Virilettes are "Caucasian females, 18–24, with no education beyond high school and entry-level service or factory jobs."

Commentators could barely hide their smirks as they listed the tractor pulls, motorcycle races, and macho-man contests that comprise the leisure activities of the target group. Crocodile tears flowed copiously. "It's blue-collar people without enough education to understand what is happening to them," mourned Virginia Ernster of the University of California School of Medicine. "It's pathetic that these companies would work so hard to get these women who may not feel much control over their lives." George Will, winner of the metaphor-man contest, wrote: "They use sophisticated marketing like a sniper's rifle, drawing beads on the most vulnerable, manipulable Americans." (I would walk a mile to see Virginia Ernster riding on the back of George Will's motorcycle.)

Smoking is the only evil that cannot be blamed on white males. Red men started it, but nobody will say so because that would be racist. Meanwhile, smokers are the only people in America who are subject to de jure segregation.

* * *

Here lie I, Timon, who alive all living men did hate;
Pass by and curse thy fill, but pass,
And stay not here thy gait.

Carving "Go Away" on his tombstone is guaranteed to make a misanthrope feel better about himself. One who actually did it was a citizen of ancient Athens who makes a brief appearance in Plutarch's *Lives,* the source for Shakespeare's *Timon of Athens.*

The play opens with the rich, neurotically nice Timon, "that honourable, complete, free-hearted gentleman," practicing the "untirable and continuate goodness" for which he is famed. In the course of a single morning, he adds to a girl's dowry so her beloved's father will consent to the match, sends his servants hither and yon with cash gifts to all who have touched him for a loan, and pays a friend's debts to get him out of debtor's prison. Believing that "we are born to do benefits," he throws regular banquets for the deadbeats of Athens, who are steadily eating him out of house and home.

His only real friend is a good-natured cynic named Apemantus who lives by the Golden Mean that Timon so ostentatiously ignores. Apemantus's opinion of human nature is contained in the table grace he recites by way of warning at one of the banquets.

> Immortal gods, I crave no pelf;
> I pray for no man but myself;
> Grant I may never prove so fond
> To trust man on his oath or bond,
> Or a harlot for her weeping,
> Or a dog that seems a-sleeping,
> Or a keeper with my freedom,
> Or my friends if I should need 'em.
> Amen. So fall to it.

But Timon pays no attention to this shrewd advice. When the debtor that he sprang from jail tries to pay him back, he refuses to hear of it, saying, "I gave it freely ever." Taking him at his word, his other so-called friends don't bother to pay him back either. Nor do they come to his rescue when he finally goes bankrupt.

Realizing that he has been betrayed, Timon throws one last banquet for the freeloaders. Thinking that he has somehow recouped his fortunes, they all show up in their usual expectant mood, but this night they are greeted by the New Timon.

"You knot of mouth-friends!" he screams, and then uncovers the platters. Dinner is warm water and stones.

"Live loathed and long," he tells them, calling them "smiling, smooth, detested parasites, courteous destroyers, affable wolves, meek bears, trencher-friends and minute-jacks." Then he really lets loose:

> *"Burn house! sink Athens! henceforth hated be*
> *Of Timon man and all humanity!"*

We next meet him outside the walls of Athens, where he enumerates the calamities he hopes will strike the city: adulterous wives, disobedient children, thieving servants, slave uprisings, "itches, blains, and leprosy," and sons who "pluck the lined crutch from thy old limping sire, and with it beat out his brains."

He himself won't be there to see it, however:

> *"Timon will to the woods, where he shall find*
> *The unkindest beast more kinder than mankind. . . .*
> *And grant, as Timon grows, his hate may grow*
> *To the whole race of mankind, high and low."*

He becomes a hermit. When his still-loyal steward comes to visit him, he tells the man:

> *"Hate all, curse all, show charity to none,*
> *But let the famished flesh slide from the bone*

> *Ere thou relieve the beggar. Give to dogs*
> *What thou deniest to men. Let prisons swallow 'em."*

Alcibiades has no better luck. "I am Misanthropos, and hate mankind," Timon tells him. "For thy part, I do wish thou wert a dog."

Apemantus the Cynic makes the trek out to the hermitage to try and talk some sense into him. "The middle of humanity thou never knewest, but the extremity of both ends," the wise old man says, but it does no good.

Next, Timon is visited by a delegation of senators. With seeming hospitality he gives them a tour of his hermitage and asks them to take a message back to the citizens of Athens. The senators perk up, thinking he must be feeling better, but this, according to Plutarch, is what he said:

"I have a little yard where there grows a fig tree on which many citizens have hanged themselves. And, because I mean to make some building on the place, I thought it good to let you all understand that, before the tree be cut down, if any of you be desperate, you may there go hang yourselves."

Shortly afterwards Timon himself dies and is laid to rest under his notorious tombstone. Knowing that the curious will ignore the inscription and come anyway, he spent his last days landscaping the spot in such a way that the weight of the crowd will cause it to sink into the sea.

Timon of Athens is universally acknowledged to be Shakespeare's worst play: "two plays, casually joined at the middle," according to Mark Van Doren. Some scholars suspect that the version we have was actually a rough draft that Shakespeare put aside, intending to polish it later, but never got around to it. Others think Shakespeare wrote half of it and somebody else finished it. Whatever happened, the dramatic fault is lack of foreshadowing. The protagonist swings from one extreme to the other with such speed and clumsy motivation that audiences can't believe in it.

The only way to salvage it is to turn it into a screenplay called *Regarding Timon.* Once it's billed as "an American story for the 90's" it will make perfect sense.

THE GOADING
OF AMERICA

Fisher Ames is the Founding Father who draws a blank. When I first discussed the idea for this book with my agent and various editors, none of them had ever heard of him, and neither had any of the people who volunteered the names of their favorite misanthropes.

I told them not to feel bad. I was a history major through graduate school, with A's in *American Revolution* and *U.S. Constitution,* but until a few years ago when I came across him in my private reading, I had never heard of Fisher Ames either.

Yet it was Ames who wrote the final version of the First Amendment, and his speech on Jay's Treaty, delivered when he was the leader of the Federalists in the First Congress, was called the finest example of American oratory by Daniel Webster and Abraham Lincoln, both of whom memorized large portions of it to train themselves in the art.

Why then the blackout on Fisher Ames?

He was born in Dedham, Massachusetts in 1758, entered Harvard at twelve, and graduated at sixteen. After teaching himself law, he went into practice, farming the family lands on the side, until politics called.

The Ames home seems to have been a cocoon of idyllic happiness. His wife evinced none of the nascent feminism of Abigail Adams. She gave him six sons and a daughter, who received large chunks of paternal quality time thanks to the pleasure Ames took in inventing and playing educational games. He also got along well with his in-laws; his letters to brother-in-law Thomas Dwight are as warm as they are voluminous.

Fisher Ames was called a "sweet" man by his contemporaries. His first biographer, writing shortly after his death, spoke of "the charms of his conversation and manners [that] won affection" and "the delicacy, the ardor, and constancy with which he cherished his friends," and said: "He had a perfect command of his temper; his anger never proceeded to passion, nor his sense of injury to revenge."

No one sounds less like a misanthrope, yet Fisher Ames had a bleak opinion of human nature. "Our mistake is in supposing men better than they are. They are bad, and will act their character out," he wrote. He insured his absence from history textbooks with: "Our disease is democracy. Democracy is a troubled spirit, fated never to rest, and whose dreams, if it sleeps, present only visions of hell."

Ames's fellow Federalist and philosophical soulmate, Alexander Hamilton, held the same views and just as frequently aired them. It being impossible, however, to ignore Hamilton in the textbooks, it has been the custom to soft-pedal his opinions of mankind and democracy—e.g., the typical high school or college text will say, "Hamilton distrusted the people," when in fact he said: "The people! The people, sir, are a great beast!"

45

Both Ames and Hamilton, and in a later era Henry Adams, were sociable men with a wide circle of friends who nonetheless qualify for conditional membership in the ranks of misanthropy. As Federalists, Ames and Hamilton believed in a government controlled by "the wise, the rich, and the good," the same philosophy held by Henry Adams, who was nominally a Democrat. The views of all three men amounted to what we now call elitism. Since the elitist hates the masses, and since the masses make up the vast majority of the human race, the elitist conservative is, numerically speaking, a practicing misanthrope.

In Ames's case, his basic outlook was exacerbated by a political event that goaded him into a bitter hatred of mankind. It is no exaggeration to say that he was frightened into misanthropy by the French Revolution.

As word of the excesses of the Terror filtered in—summary executions, blood-drinking, cannibalism, massacres of nuns, the sexual dismemberment of the Princess de Lamballe, accusations of incest against Marie Antoinette—all done in the name of "the People," Ames coined the word "mobocracy" and likened France to "a Cerberus gaping with ten thousand throats, all parched and thirsting for fresh blood. . . . tyranny more vindictive, unfeeling, and rapacious than that of Tiberius, Nero, or Caligula, or any single despot that ever existed."

Ames was not alone; Burke in England reacted the same way. The French Revolution probably created more misanthropes than any other event in history. In other bloodbaths the evildoers have been exotic foreign marauders or nations within nations—Huns, Bolsheviks, Nazis, Khmer Rouge—but in the France of the Terror they were *the People,* humanity's upper-case whole.

The French Revolution frightened Jefferson and his democratic republicans too, but for a very different reason. The conservative Federalists, fearing the people, wanted a strong central government with a powerful executive branch. But the liberal Jeffersonians, fearing kings, wanted separation of powers and checks and balances to control the executive, whom they saw as a potential Louis XVI ever ready to abridge the people's rights. To Ames, this amounted to a deliberate weakening of executive authority inflicted on the Constitution by those who imagined all government to be a Bourbon king.

Ames loathed Thomas Jefferson, considering him a dupe of the French Enlightenment's naive, optimistic faith in the essential goodness of human nature. Whenever anyone quoted Jefferson's "all men are created equal," Ames shot back: "but differ greatly in the sequel."

The "Jeffs," as Ames called the democratic republicans, moved him to savage eloquence: "They learn to throw their eyes beyond the gulf of revolution, confusion, and civil war, which yawns at their feet, to behold an Eden of primitive innocence equality, and liberty. . . . The rights of man are to be established by being solemnly proclaimed, and printed, so that every citizen shall have a copy. Avarice, ambition, revenge, and rage will be disenchanted from all hearts and die there; man will be regenerated. . . . and the glorious work of that perfectibility of the species, foretold by Condorcet, will begin."

To the democratic-republican claim that anarchy could be avoided by giving the people so much freedom that they would have nothing to rebel against, Ames countered that human nature being what it is, people will always find something to rebel against; if nothing else, envy will make them crave "the power to make others wretched."

He predicted the rise of what he called "factions" and we call pressure groups: "A combination of a very small minority can effectually defeat the authority of the national will. . . . Suppose at first their numbers to be exceedingly few, their efforts will for that reason be so much the greater. They will call themselves the People; they will in their name arraign every act of government as wicked and weak; they will oblige the rulers to stand forever on the defensive. . . . With a venal press at command, concealing their number and their infamy, is it to be doubted that the ignorant will soon or late unite with the vicious?"

But, the democratic republicans argued, the majority rules! No, said Ames, they don't. The price of liberty is eternal vigilance, and most people are unwilling to pay it: "The virtuous, who do not wish to control the society, but quietly to enjoy its protection; the enterprising merchant, the thriving tradesman, the careful farmer, will be engrossed by the toils of their business, and will have little time or inclination for the unprofitable and disquieting pursuit of politics."

The only eternally vigilant citizens in a democracy, Ames warned, will be members of factions whose ceaseless demands will cause "a state of agitation that is justly terrible to all who love their ease. . . . it tries and wears out the strength of the government and the temper of the people. It is a game which the factious will never be weary of playing, for conquering parties never content themselves with half the fruits of victory."

Ames opposed the addition of the Bill of Rights to the Constitution, believing that the Magna Charta guaranteed everything that needed to be guaranteed. A member of Congress when the Bill of Rights was introduced, he wrote scathingly in a letter to Thomas Dwight:

Mr. Madison has introduced his long expected amendments. They are the fruit of much labor and research. He has hunted up all the grievances and complaints of newspapers, all the articles of conventions, and the small talk of their debates. It contains a bill of rights, the right of enjoying property, of changing the government at pleasure, freedom of the press, of conscience, of juries, exemption from general warrants, gradual increase of representatives. . . . This is the substance. There is too much of it. Oh! I had forgot, the right of the people to bear arms. *Risum teneatis amici?* [Can we restrain our laughter?] Upon the whole, it may do some good towards quieting men, who attend to sounds only, and may get the mover some popularity, which he wishes.

Ames wrote the final version of the First Amendment, not because he approved of it, but simply to bring literary order to the unwieldy bundle of rights that Madison amassed.

As time went on and his health failed, Ames's bitterness increased. When Jefferson was elected president he said: "We are in the hands of the philosophers of Lilliput." As for the Louisiana Purchase, it was "a Gallo-Hispano-Indian Omnium Gatherum" destined to produce even more factions and lead us down that fatal Roman road from a republic ruled by laws to an empire ruled by power.

He continued to pound away at democracy. "What other form of civil rule so irresistibly tends to free vice from restraint and to subject virtue to persecution?" "There is universally a presumption in democracy that promises everything, and at the same time an imbecility that can accomplish nothing, not even preserve itself." "We are sliding down into the mire of a democracy, which pollutes the morals of the citizens before it swallows up their liberties."

Five years before his death he wrote Thomas Dwight: "Our country is too big for union, too sordid for patriotism, too democratic for liberty." He was glad to be out of politics: "Nor will I any longer be at the trouble to govern this country. I am no Atlas, and my shoulders ache."

In the end, he seemed to adopt a broader misanthropy extending beyond American politics to the entire race of mankind: "Indeed I consider the whole civilized world as metal thrown back into the furnace, to be melted over again."

Most people know that John Adams and Thomas Jefferson both died at a ripe age on the same day: July 4, 1826. Given the superstitious weight of the number *three,* a study of the life of Fisher Ames concludes with a chill down the spine, for Ames died of tuberculosis at age fifty on July 4, 1808.

The Grim Reaper's unhealthy interest in America's birthday takes on ominous significance when we examine our present national mood in the light of Fisher Ames's warnings about factionalism.

Our underlying fear that there is no national glue holding us together has always been embarrassingly obvious. Whenever calamity strikes—Pearl Harbor, Dallas, the Iranian hostages, the Challenger explosion—we give ourselves away with a verbal pat on the back that we recite with conspicuous relief: "It brought us together."

Collecting Gotterdammerungs in the cause of union will no longer work. There is so much pluribus in the unum that everybody is somebody's "them."

Affirmative action is our French Revolution, goading us into misanthropy as surely as the excesses of the Terror goaded Fisher Ames. It has sent a twist through the national belly, as anyone who knows anything about this country might have predicted, for when you hit Americans in the college education, you hit them where they live.

What's the use? is becoming our national war cry. Copious tears have been shed over despairing rage in the ghetto, but there's more than one kind of despairing rage, and more than one kind of ghetto. The talented student who cracks the books to get into college, only to be passed over for someone less deserving, thinks *what's the use?* and then feels the twist in the belly. His parents, who have worked themselves ragged to give him a college education, think *what's the use?* and then feel the twist in the belly. The professor who demands excellence from his students, only to find himself charged with elitism, thinks *what's the use?* and then feels the twist in the belly.

The present mood of America, especially on college campuses, recalls Robinson Jeffers's phrase, "something in the air that hates humanity." Assessing the Civil Rights Act of 1990, Thomas Sowell lays it on the line:

> I see no reason why it can't happen here. Nothing is easier than to start a spiral of racial confrontations, and nothing is harder than to stop it. . . . we will have quotas set in concrete, no matter how much people deny it. And the hatred that is going to grow out of that is going to be something like we've never seen. . . . There's a consolation in being as old as I am. I don't think that I'm going to live to see the terrible trends that are setting in, particularly in race relations, come to their conclusion. I certainly would not want to be here for that.

Affirmative action was designed originally for "women and other minorities" but the phrase has become just another tortured euphemism. Female conscientiousness and eagerness to please have always made women good students and natural test takers. Jews have gloried in scholarship throughout the ages, and Asians of both sexes score so high on SATs and IQ tests that they regard affirmative action as an impediment. Affirmative action really means favoritism for blacks for the sake of racial peace, but the favor is pure chimera, and so, increasingly, is the peace.

Hatred of truth is misanthropy in the fullest sense because it is a denial of the human spirit. Evidence that many blacks have sunk to this nadir is piling up.

In 1919 there was a popular song called "The Irish Were Egyptians Long Ago." Now a growing band of black scholars is insisting that blacks were. Calling themselves "Afrocentrists," they are demanding that curricula at all levels be rewritten to include the contributions of black Egypt. These assay out to just about everything ever invented, written, and built, for by placing themselves in ancient Egypt, blacks can thus claim that they antedated and influenced ancient Greece, and take credit for all the seminal discoveries in mathematics, architecture, sculpture, astronomy, and philosophy that make up Western civilization.

This is precisely what they are doing. The leading Egyptomaniacs—Martin Bernal of Cornell, Asa G. Hilliard III of Georgia State, Theophile J. Obenga of Gabon—contend that Greek philosophers "sat at the feet" of black Egyptian priests, who taught them all they knew. Hilliard also claims that Rameses, King Tut, Moses, Cleopatra, Jesus, Buddha, and Aesop were black or partly so; and that study at "the great African universities" was "fairly common" among the ancestors of American slaves. He concludes: "Since Africa is widely believed to be the birthplace of the human race, it follows that Africa was the birthplace of mathematics and science." *It follows?* If geometry and structural engineering had been based on that kind of logic, the pyramids would have collapsed on the Jewish slaves that the black Egyptians presumably owned.

The most outlandish claim comes from an Oregon teacher, Carolyn Leonard, who has solved the riddle of the Sphinx: "Napoleon shot off its nose to alter the facial features so people wouldn't know it was African." This happened to a lot of old statues, according to Leonard. "They were not eroded by time, but deliberately altered to rid them of the vestiges of African features."

Afrocentrism is catching on. Sphinxologist Leonard is ensconced in the Portland school system with the glorious title of Coordinator of the Multicultural-Multiethnic Education Office. The New York State Department of Education has created a new "curriculum of inclusion," and in Washington, D.C. a former sixties activist, Albena Walker, is conducting an elementary school "pilot program." According to the *Washington Times,* her curriculum employs yoga. ("In through the noses, out through the mouths. . . . all the spiritual sciences have their roots in Africa. . . . Invoke your ancestors, breathe in, breathe out").

John Leo of *U.S. News & World Report* calls Afrocentrism "a sort of Tawana Brawley theory of history, in which facts do not matter, only resentments and group solidarity." However, Leo adds that when he called seven prominent Egyptologists at random to ask their opinion on the Black Egypt theory, all seven said it was not true—"then asked that their names not be used." One told him it was "politically too hot" to get into.

Egyptologists tend to be dependent on grants from foundations, which are dependent on government tax laws. Most people erudite enough to dispute Afrocentrism are sucking on some public or semi-public tit, which explains why only four scholars so far have come forward to do battle. Two of them are unassailable emeriti of history almost as eternal as the pyramids themselves: Henry Steele Commager and Arthur J. Schlesinger, Jr. The other two are William H. McNeill and Diane Ravitch, who was called "Miss Daisy" by the offended Egyptomaniacs.

The four have formed the Committee of Scholars in Defense of History, but who will be brave enough to lend them public support? Certainly not the enterprising merchant, the thriving tradesman, the careful farmer, or the rest of our virtuous citizenry who do not wish to control society, but quietly to enjoy its protection and send their children to its schools. They, who have little time or inclination for the unprofitable and disquieting task of being called racists, will simply grumble in private until they wake up one morning and find that Afro Ed has become a required course in every school in America, and nobody will know how it happened.

A further indication that blacks as a group are becoming misanthropic is their increasingly testy readiness to regard as white anyone who is not black.

Miami is a flashpoint for black-Hispanic tensions. Black accusations of brutality against Hispanic police pulsate with the same frenzied quality of similar cases against white police in the sixties. They also are showing the same tendency to turn into causes célèbres, such as last year's well-publicized trial of an Hispanic officer who shot a black motorcyclist who tried to run him over. The Miami police force itself has divided along racial lines: black officers have charged that Hispanic officers are slow to respond to back-up calls from them.

In "Hispanics vs. Blacks in Houston," about the ongoing struggle for municipal power, *Newsweek* reporter Ginny Carroll writes: "The reigning assumption seems to be that the nation's two largest minorities will have to duke it out, while white control remains intact. . . . the animus between [Hispanics] and Houston blacks is likely to worsen."

Black hostility toward Asians has mounted steadily in the face of Asian business success, which many inner-city blacks attribute to a government plot, and the superior academic performance of Asian students in tests that are supposedly biased in favor of whites.

A personality conflict freighted with irony has also emerged. Explaining what it is about Asians that blacks don't like, the embattled Korean grocer whose Brooklyn store has been the target of a year-long black boycott told the *Washington Post:* "Because we don't laugh so much and don't smile so much, it doesn't seem like we're very kind people." Blacks are now demanding smiling good cheer of Asians just as white Southerners once demanded it of them.

Black anti-Semitism has been around a long time but it entered new realms when Toni Morrison told *Time:* "What I find is a lot of black people who believe that Jews in this country, by and large, have become white. They behave like white people rather than Jewish people."

Rachel Flick confronted the same attitude at a 1988 black-Jewish conference in Atlanta convened to repair the damage between the two groups. "What emerged in Atlanta, moreover, was that interest in repairing the alliance is one-sided," said Flick. "For Jews of the Reform tradition, as most of the civil-rights activists are, an alliance with the downtrodden is an essential part of feeling Jewish. But for blacks, Jews are white—a point tactfully and truthfully offered by Benjamin Hooks of the National Association for the Advancement of Colored People."

As a final fillip, blacks have thrown down the gauntlet to feminists. To repair the damage done to poor black males by their female-dominated, fatherless environments, the growing movement by black educators to segregate boys into separate classes, or even separate schools staffed exclusively by black male teachers, can only undermine the whole concept of sexual equality and re-invent Freudianism, complete with new-old buzz-words like "emasculation."

Hispanics, Asians, Jews, women—blacks are flailing their way into misanthropy minority by minority, group by group, faction by faction. If it continues, our Omnium Gatherum might well achieve a unity nobody bargained for.

A few years ago, while having coffee in my favorite diner, I eavesdropped on a conversation between two good ole boys who were discussing the race for the 1984 Democratic presidential nomination. This is what I overheard:

"Hey, T. J., you know whut?"

"Whuzzat, Dwayne?"

"If the Jews hate Jesse Jackson, they cain't be too bad."

Political scientists would call this a re-alignment but in fact it is a movement of the earth. When Dwayne and T. J. become good ole goys, anything can happen. If blacks continue on their misanthropic way they will eventually goad the rest of the population into a monolithic "white" race. The concept of ethnicity will vanish altogether as Hispanics join other whites in adopting the Eurocentrism of which we presently stand accused. Asians, having given "Protestant Ethic" new meaning with their thrift and hard work, will increasingly think of themselves, and be thought of, as white—as they already are at the Virginia State Employment Commission, which lumps them with whites in the category called "Other."

There is no telling where it will end, though I am willing to venture a guess: Wasps will finally stop describing as "foreign looking" anyone who does not turn pink and blister after an hour in the sun.

TENDER
MISANTHROPES

The word *misanthrope* ought to be inhospitable to qualification and immune to modifiers, but it isn't. Misanthropes come in two models that were defined by the literary historian Irving Babbitt in his monumental 1919 work, *Rousseau and Romanticism.* "The tender misanthropy of the Rousseauist," Babbitt wrote, "is at the opposite pole from that of a Swift, which is the misanthropy of the naked intellect."

The misanthrope of the naked intellect hates people straight down the line with no exceptions and no regrets. Regarding mankind as hopeless, he tends to be apolitical. Regarding mankind as loathsome, he tends to be an apolitical arch-conservative, a purely temperamental stance whose sole purpose is hands-off, apocalyptic revenge. Presented with Thomas Hobbes's assessment, "The life of man is solitary, poor, nasty, brutish, and short," he replies: "If it ain't broke, don't fix it."

The tender misanthrope, on the other hand, despises humanity

in general but is ever ready to make an exception for the *real*
people. He feels certain that he could love them if only he could
find them—or failing that, transform existing false people into
his idealized *real* people through social and political programs of
his own making.

The world has endured regular bouts of tender misanthropy.
The worst upheaval occurred in the fifth century, when early
Christian hermits fled to the deserts of North Africa and became
their own *real* people. In the early twentieth century, tender
misanthropes decided that the *real* people were "the Workers,"
while to the tender misanthropes of eighteenth-century France,
the *real* people were "noble savages."

Jean-Jacques Rousseau's *Discourse on the Origins of Inequality*
praised "natural man" over his civilized counterpart, who, he
believed, had been ruined by knowledge, culture, luxury, and
"insincere" polished manners. Civilization, said Rousseau, really
ought to be torn down and all laws abolished so that everybody
could be happy like the simple peasants who placed heart over
head, emotion over logic, nature over culture, soul over all.

He sent Voltaire a copy of the *Discourse* but the grand old
cynic, who was a bona fide liberal, saw through Rousseau's
misanthropic liberalism and took a dig at him in his thank-you
note: "I have received, sir, your new book against the human
species, and I thank you for it. No one has ever been so witty as
you are in trying to turn us into brutes; to read your book makes
one long to go on all fours. As, however, it is now some sixty
years since I gave up the practice, I feel that it is unfortunately
impossible for me to resume it."

Jean-Jacques Rousseau was born in Geneva in 1712 to a forty-
year-old mother who died two days later. His father was a watch-
maker with aristocratic pretensions that he expressed by wearing

a sword and keeping it on the equivalent of hair-trigger, resulting in several incarcerations for public brawling.

Jean-Jacques also had aristocratic pretensions but they went beyond his father's simpleminded pleasure in swashbuckling. "What was hardest to destroy in me," he wrote later, "was a proud misanthropy, a certain acrimony against the rich and happy of the world as though they were so at my expense, as though their alleged happiness had been usurped from mine."

Apprenticed to an engraver, he hated the common atmosphere of the workshop so much that he ran away, becoming a nomadic Jack-of-all-trades and, whenever possible, an older woman's kept boy. His relationship with his first patroness, Mme de Warens, is summed up by his pet name for her: *"Maman."*

The ad hoc quality of Rousseau's mind and the hysteria that lay just under the surface of his personality emerge in the story he told of how he came to be a writer. In 1749 as he was walking along the Vincennes road on his way to visit Diderot in prison, he happened to buy a newspaper in which he happened to see a notice that the Dijon Academy was holding an essay contest on the influence of formal manners on French culture. What happened next sounds very much like a fit:

"All at once I felt myself dazzled by a thousand sparkling lights; crowds of vivid ideas thronged into my head with a force and confusion that threw me into unspeakable agitation; I felt my head whirling in a giddiness like that of intoxication." He sat down under a tree, ideas surging through his fevered brain. At last, when he had pulled himself together, he saw that his shirt-front was wet with tears but could not remember having shed them.

He wrote the essay, won the prize, and wormed his way into the homes of bored French aristocrats, becoming the last word in radical chic. Ensconced as the man of the hour, he turned out a plethora of how-to and self-help treatises on subjects ranging from botany to solitary hikes to breastfeeding. He was notoriously a tit man, but instead of admitting it to himself and accepting it as one of life's more pleasurable hang-ups, he rationalized it in the same way that he rationalized his misanthropy, writing and talking so much about primitive scenes, mother's milk, and peasant warmth that breastfeeding became a national fad, even among women of the nobility who had always used wet nurses.

His concern did not extend to his mistress, the scullery maid Thérèse Vasseur, who had given birth to five children by him. Having gained an entrée into Parisian society, he did not want to advertise his connection with the common Thérèse, so he dumped all five little ads in a foundling home and then wrote a book on how to raise children. *Emile,* as it was called, laid out a program of "natural" behavior over rigid discipline, "natural" environments over artificial ones, and "freedom" from stifling rules.

In quick succession came a romantic novel, *La Nouvelle Héloise,* equating sincerity of feeling with manic depression ("I love you as one must love, with excess, madness, rapture and despair"), and a political treatise, *The Social Contract* ("Man is born free but he is everywhere in chains"). After that the Establishment had had enough; Rousseau's books were condemned by church and state and their author exiled.

He lived for a while in England where he met David Hume, with whom he soon broke over some imagined offense, and young James Boswell, who visited him at his next place of exile in Switzerland. They had dinner in Rousseau's kitchen, served by the long-suffering Thérèse Vasseur, who had stuck with him despite the disappearing act he performed with their children. The visit ended abruptly when Rousseau snapped at Boswell,

"You are irksome to me. I cannot help it, it's my nature. Go away."

Boswell was the last man to see him before he went completely round the bend. Two weeks later, Voltaire published a pamphlet poking fun at *Héloise* and revealing the story of the five abandoned children. Thereafter a broken man, Rousseau suffered regular delusions of persecution until his death in 1778.

He was buried on the estate of one of his hard-core fans, the Marquis de Girardin, a forerunner of today's limousine liberals, who planted him on the "Isle of Poplars" in the middle of a lake, the gravesite surmounted by an imposing tomb and surrounded by benches reserved for nursing mothers. His death triggered a new round of sentimental hysteria as thousands of pilgrims (including Marie Antoinette) flocked to his grave, and Elvis-like sightings of him were reported in the press. Fifteen years later during the Reign of Terror, the Jacobins, who rode to power on the primitivism he unleashed, reburied him in the Pantheon where he still lies.

Rousseau's philosophy can be summed up by the buzzword of his day: *sensibilité*—what our age calls "getting in touch with your feelings." His methodology can be summed up by the title of Johnny Ray's 1952 hit song: "Cry."

Rousseauian tears, says Simon Schama in *Citizens,* were regarded as "the soul directly irrigating the countenance. More important, a good fit of crying indicated that the child had been miraculously preserved within the man or woman. So Rousseau's heroes and heroines, beginning with himself, sob, weep and blubber at the slightest provocation."

The *sensibilité* craze spread to other arts. The philosopher Diderot, one of the Encyclopedists, also endorsed coming apart: "Move me, astonish me, unnerve me, make me tremble, weep, shudder and rage." A favorite painter of the time, Jean-Baptiste

FLORENCE KING

Greuze, the Rousseau of the palette, had all of Paris in a sodden mess with his *Girl Weeping Over Her Dead Canary*. An art critic wrote that he went back again and again to gaze at it and cry some more: "I have passed whole hours in attentive contemplation so that I became drunk with a sweet and tender sadness."

According to Rousseau, the best place to cry was in the woods. Nature was particularly well-suited to his overwrought vocabulary. The woods were *wild, untamed, primitive, lush*. The woods were full of *nooks, copses, verdant canopies, umbrageous illusions*. They were also full of sobbing Rousseau fans but never mind that, you could be *alone with nature* in the woods, *lose yourself* in their beauty, *let it wash over you*, sleep *naked* in a *bower* and *become as one* with nature's *torrents*. Afterwards, you could write about your sylvan crying jag and claim to be *drunk with* emotion, a cliché that is with us still.

To understand why eighteenth-century France succumbed to his glorification of unbuttoned hysteria, it is necessary to know what seventeenth-century France had been like. Called the Age of Reason, it was a neoclassical period that modeled its behavior on the stern virtues of Early Rome: honor, duty, courage, and especially *gravitas*, that dignified stoicism in the face of personal pain that was considered the mark of an aristocrat.

In literature and drama these virtues were transmuted into simple logical plots faithful to the Aristotelian model, pithy epigrams modeled on Martial, a reverence for linguistic precision as dictated by the Académie Française, a lofty formalism requiring actors to declaim rather than emote, and a curtain of charity prohibiting scenes of lust and violence from the stage.

In life as in art, the watchwords were self-control and decorum. Rigid perhaps, but Frenchmen of the seventeenth century had a high opinion of human nature and a limitless faith in

Man's capacity for rational behavior. We get from people what we demand of them and the Age of Reason demanded much.

The neoclassicists did not deny emotions altogether. One of their leading lights, Blaise Pascal, penned the famous line, "The heart has its reasons of which reason knows nothing," but he said it and got out, leaving posterity an exquisitely balanced epigram. Rousseau said it and kept on saying it over and over in purple prose until his followers were as conditioned as Pavlov's dogs. If he did not actually cause the French Revolution, he certainly set it up. His message of *I feel, therefore I am* ushered in a self-indulgent emotionalism that spilled over into political anarchy and became the rationale for the Reign of Terror.

Only a tender misanthrope could screw up the world as Rousseau did. The misanthrope of the naked intellect, disdaining such categories as *real* people on the grounds that if indeed they exist, they must be even worse than the other kind, has no wish to liberate the repressions of a species that he already finds intolerable. If he must share the world with people, he wants them to be as decorous and self-controlled as possible. He is thus an Age of Reason unto himself who, for purely selfish motives, places humanity on a pedestal and holds it to the highest standard of behavior. Ironically or not, the misanthrope of the naked intellect is the true friend of mankind.

By contrast, humanity has never regained the dignity and strength of character that Rousseau's tender misanthropy destroyed. His glorification of "natural" behavior foretold the Freudian theory of repression which encouraged man to regard his conscience as his worst enemy, leading in turn to the hippie credos of "Let it all hang out" and "If it feels good, do it," and the coarse sexual honesty that the seventies called "getting down and dirty."

And now we have "out of control," a trendy euphemism describing the behavior of someone who has sunk below the rational level and entered the realm of dark impulse. Bret Easton Ellis's *American Psycho* would have sounded very familiar to the Paris mob that cut out the vulva of the Princess de Lamballe, stuck it on a pike, and held it up to Marie Antoinette's window amid howling demands that she kiss it. They also did the same things that Jeffrey Dahmer did in his gory Milwaukee apartment—except that he did them in secret and they did them in the middle of the Place de la Concorde in broad daylight because they had been saturated, trickle-down fashion, in a Rousseauian ethos that urged them to abandon their unique human capacities for rationalism and civilized behavior and surrender themselves to primitive instinct.

Seeing how much American madness can be traced back to Jean-Jacques Rousseau is like seeing how many words can be formed from *antidisestablishmentarianism.* In both cases the answer is: a lot.

The phrase "pursuit of happiness" has a suspiciously Rousseauian ring, as well it might. The well-read Thomas Jefferson was his contemporary, and served as Minister to France in the period just after his death. The various self-realization and human-potential movements that have shredded our social fabric in the name of "feeling good about myself" are outgrowths of the oxymoronic mass individualism that Rousseau promoted in his posthumously published *Confessions,* which contains the Western world's first mantra: "I am not made like anyone I have seen; I dare believe that I am not made like anyone in existence. If I am not better, at least I am different."

Real people are everywhere now: beating drums in the woods in New Man weekend pow-wows, mooning coeds on campuses, simulating pelvic thrusts under the goal posts, leaping naked out of the stands to steal home plate, and letting unleashed emotions wash over them in today's version of the verdant canopy, the confessional talk show. The cheapness, tawdriness, and utter lack of class that ooze out of Oprah, Donahue, and Geraldo are the recycled *sensibilité* of Jean-Jacques Rousseau, the tender misanthrope who loved people so much that he dumped human dignity in a foundling home.

"A special type of sincerity," wrote Irving Babbitt, "is itself an outcome of the Rousseauistic movement. It seems to be assumed in certain quarters that almost any opinion is justified provided it be held with sufficient emotional vehemence." Homeless advocate Mitch Snyder, who abandoned his wife and children so he could take care of strangers, was vehemently sincere. The self-analysis he gave to a Washington reporter shortly before committing suicide could be slipped into an edition of Rousseau's *Confessions* with no one the wiser—including Rousseau.

> I don't consider myself a good person. I tend to be very impatient,
> I tend to be very short, I tend to make heavy demands on people.
> I don't have much time or energy to give much one-on-one, and
> so I'm very hard on people around me. I take much more than I
> give. I give to people in the shelter, I give to people on the streets,
> I give to people who are suffering, but that's got little to do with
> people who are around me. They pay the price.

"The misanthropist of the Rousseauistic or Byronic type has a resource that was denied to Swift," Irving Babbitt continues. "Having failed to find companionship among men he can flee to nature."

Green grow the Rousseaus, O! Anyone who has received junk mail from Greenpeace has read Jean-Jacques in full throttle: "Listening to 500 dolphins shrieking in panic as they fight and gasp for air. . . . standing by helplessly as living dolphins were dragged aloft thrashing and flailing in terror. . . ." Suddenly, I awoke in the Fredericksburg post office to find tears on the front of my Baltimore Orioles warm-up jacket, yet I had no memory of having shed them.

The current crop of rat lovers, cockroach cuddlers, and assorted environ-mental cases never come right out and say "I am a misanthrope." They prefer to hate human nature through what Babbitt called "an Arcadian haze."

Typical is a letter in the *Santa Barbara News-Press* from one Charles LeCompte: "Think how nice this planet would be with no humans. The air would be super-clean, the oceans super-clean. But no! Humans came along with their ignorance and greed and have just about destroyed this planet. Depending on personal beliefs, God or nature made one big mistake, and that mistake is humans."

Or try this helpful hint from *Earth First! Journal:* "Are you terminally ill with a wasting disease? Don't go out with a whimper; go out with a bang! Undertake an eco-kamikaze mission. . . . The possibilities are limitless. Dams . . . are crying out to be blown to smithereens, as are industrial polluters, the headquarters of oil-spilling corporations, fur warehouses, paper mills. . . . To those feeling suicidal, this may be the answer to your dreams. . . . Don't jump off a bridge, blow up a bridge. Who says you can't take it with you?"

I frankly admit I like that. As a child I was powerfully influenced by Veronica Lake's heroic deed in the World War II movie about Bataan nurses, *So Proudly We Hail,* when she walked into a Japanese barracks with a grenade tucked in her bra. The lustful grinning soldiers surrounded her, and then. . . .

I saw it when I was in elementary school, when the first of many progressive teachers was riding me about being antisocial.

Thereafter, whenever I was accused of aloofness, a picture of Veronica Lake rose in my mind. *They want me to have more extracurricular activities, huh? They want me to join clubs, huh? They want me to go to group functions, huh? Okey-dokey. . . .*

This is definitely a misanthrope's fantasy. *Earth First!* won't tell you; I just did.

The rise of the animal-rights movement has been attributed to "post-industrial" this-and-that but I detect several quasi-misanthropic causes.

Liberals have developed compassion fatigue for their own species but they are too liberal to say so.

The now-famous war cry, "a rat is a pig is a dog is a boy," is simply another way of saying that we have run out of humans to demand rights for. Equality was bound to come to this.

Animal-rights activism gives disillusioned feminists an excuse to go back to being women protecting wee creatures without compromising their radical credentials.

Animal-rights activists are motivated by an unconscious wish to escape the sexual revolution through the evocation of chaste childhood images of a boy and his dog or a girl and her horse.

Like Rousseau, they are hypocritical snobs. Fisher Ames and Alexander Hamilton were honest about their hatred of the masses, as were Sir Harold Nicholson ("I hate the common people"), and John Randolph of Roanoke ("I am an aristocrat. I hate equality, I love liberty"). But the quadruphiles couch their class hatred in jokes about polyester and testimonials to natural fabrics, which they invariably anthropomorphize: cotton "breathes," madras "bleeds" (leather used to do something or other before they swore off it).

They are the same people who sang "We Are the World" but it ought to be "We Are the Graduate School." According to the frequently published statistic, 99 percent of quadruphiles are white, 51 percent are college graduates, 36 percent have done post-graduate work, and a third earn at least $40,000 a year. This means they are "articulate." Articulate? *Speciesism?* Fittingly, you have to have a harelip to pronounce it.

"I detest my fellow-beings and do not feel that I am their fellow at all," wrote Gustave Flaubert.

Flaubert (1821–1880) is France's misanthrope of the naked intellect who turned the literary tables on the tender misanthropy of Jean-Jacques Rousseau.

He was born in Rouen at the mid-point of the Romantic Movement that Rousseau spawned, an era of palmy neuroticism when the affliction of choice was *Sturm und Drang* and the beau ideal was a dead poet, preferably under thirty.

The Romantics were round-the-clock free spirits. Coleridge turned on to opium and Wordsworth bemoaned the invention of railroads because they discouraged vagabondism. Many Romantics led such hectic personal lives that it is hard to see how they managed to get any work done. George Sand left her husband and put on pants, the better to chase Frédéric Chopin, of whom Mme de Staël said: "The only constant thing about him was his cough." Percy Bysshe Shelley was a monster of irresponsibility whose headlong search for universal love made everyone in his orbit miserably unhappy—even including the donkeys he acquired for a trans-Alpine trip with Mary Godwin, when everything that could go wrong did go wrong due to his contempt for bourgeois habits such as planning ahead and thinking things through.

Next to suicide, the spectacle of insanity exerted the most fervid pull on the romantic imagination. The heroine of Sir Walter Scott's *The Bride of Lammermoor* went mad on her wedding night. The period's best-known literary mistress was mad to begin with, as Lord Byron discovered when he tangled with the congenitally beset, self-dramatizing Lady Caroline Lamb, who slashed her wrists at the dinner table. The fad for delirium and brain fever pervaded the recently invented Gothic novels and upped the ante on Rousseau's woods: now they were full of *stygian mists* and *melancholy penumbra.*

None of this suited Gustave Flaubert's practical, easily irritated Norman soul. He was quintessentially middle class, a doctor's son who set out to be a lawyer. When he gave up the law for writing there was no question of starving in a cold garret *à la bohème.* He lived in his family's spacious country home near Rouen with his doting widowed mother, waited on hand and foot by her and a devoted female servant who arranged the household to accommodate his need for solitude and silence.

Visits to Paris to partake of the literary ambience left him overwrought. "Contact with the world, with which I have been steadily rubbing shoulders now for fourteen months, makes me feel more and more like returning to my shell," he wrote his mother. "I hate the crowd, the herd. It seems to me always atrociously stupid or vile."

Life back home also presented problems: "I took a walk in Rouen this afternoon and met three or four Rouennais," he confided to his journal. "The sight of their vulgarity and of their very hats and overcoats, the things they said and the sound of their voices made me feel like vomiting and weeping all at once. Never since I have been in this world have I felt so suffocated by a disgust for mankind!"

He had a mistress, Louise Colet, but she got on his nerves, so he saw her only when the demands of the flesh gave him no choice. The rest of the time she had to be content with the only kind of affection that misanthropes are good at. "The most successful love affairs are conducted entirely by post," said

FLORENCE KING

George Bernard Shaw. And so Flaubert wrote letter after letter to poor Louise who, because she never understood him, assumed that the voluminous correspondence meant that he could not live without her.

She got a taste of the misanthropic point of view when she wrote him that she thought she was pregnant. He replied: "The idea of giving birth to someone fills me with horror. I'd curse myself if I became a father." He enlarged upon the point after her fears had proved false: "This paternity would have made me fall into the ordinary conditions of life. My virginity, with respect to the world, would have been wiped out, and I would have sunk into the abyss of common misery."

That misanthropes are literary classicists is axiomatic but Flaubert didn't know it yet. Determined to master the romantic style, and able to afford leisurely, material-gathering travel, he took an extended trip to the Near East to soak up some Oriental exoticism. After visiting Early Christian sites in North Africa, he returned to Rouen and wrote *The Temptation of St. Anthony,* a long, lush, lyrical fantasia full of demons, meditations, and visions.

He insisted upon reading the six-hundred-page manuscript aloud to a captive audience of two friends. It took four days, and by the time it was over they were in worse shape than St. Anthony. The book was crammed with vivid descriptions and meticulous detail but it did not "move"; the plotless story was as flat and static as its protagonist, who was a psychotic hermit.

At this Maalox moment in literary history, one of Flaubert's friends suddenly remembered a recent local scandal. "Throw it in the fire," he said of St. Anthony, "and write a novel about that doctor's wife who killed herself."

At first Flaubert didn't want to do it, but he soon realized that this stark domestic tragedy was a perfect vehicle for a misanthropic author. The story of a woman enslaved by cheap sentiment and puerile romantic dreams, *Madame Bovary* demanded a writer able to remain aloof from the emotions he had to describe. To "identify" with Emma Bovary, to weep and wallow with her in Rousseauian fashion, would have dragged both author and story down to her level and turned the book into the same sort of trashy melodramatic novel that Emma herself read and identified with.

Flaubert wrote *Madame Bovary* like a bookkeeper looking for a penny. His detachment, his objectivity, his emotional restraint, his pitiless insight and savage realism gave her the sympathy and understanding she craved and put her in a class with Andromeda.

He was equally kind to his readers. Unlike the Romantics, who believed that a writer should forget about grammar and spelling and "just let it come," Flaubert was too rigid to confuse writing with vomiting. He spent whole days searching for *"le mot juste,"* the right word, the perfect word, the *only* word that would express exactly what he wanted to say.

He always cut more than he saved. The misanthrope's abruptness finds a friend in the classicist's economy of expression. It is easy to imagine how Rousseau would have written the arsenic scene; Flaubert's laconic sentences twist like short-bladed knives: "She opened the jar and began to eat it" and "Still there was the taste of ink."

There is no such thing as a bad translation of *Madame Bovary* because it is so clear and concise that no translator could possibly go off the rails. Yet the language is so simple, the sentences are so direct, the scenes are so logically arranged around unifying points, that anyone with a few years of French under his belt can read it with ease in the original, even when schooldays are long in the past.

Madame Bovary, the work of a misanthrope, is the most user-friendly novel ever written.

YOUR PRESIDENT IS
NOT A MISANTHROPE!

Ask any American his opinion of Richard Nixon and you will get an answer as complex and contorted as Nixon himself. The French, on the other hand, respond with childlike simplicity: they're crazy about him. Small wonder, since they know him so well. The "real Nixon" has been a fixture at the Comédie Française since 1666. His name is Alceste, and he's the protagonist of Molière's play, *Le Misanthrope*.

In the Paris of Louis XIV, where style and form are everything, Alceste is notorious for his charmlessness and gaucherie.

> *The soul God gave me isn't of the sort*
> *That prospers in the weather of a court.*
> *It's all too obvious that I don't possess*
> *The virtues necessary for success.*
> *My one great talent is for speaking plain;*
> *I've never learned to flatter or to feign;*

And anyone so stupidly sincere
Had best not seek a courtier's career.

In 1948, Alceste Nixon came face to face with the kind of man he hated when Alger Hiss was called to testify before the House Un-American Activities Committee, of which Alceste was a member.

"Hiss," Alceste wrote later, "was a striking representative of the fashionable Eastern establishment—a graduate of Harvard Law School, clerk to a Supreme Court Justice, an aide to Franklin D. Roosevelt at the Yalta conference and one of the major organizers of the United Nations conference in San Francisco. He had impeccable social and intellectual qualifications, and the list of people who he said would vouch for his character ranged from Adlai E. Stevenson to John Foster Dulles. He, in effect, pleaded innocence by association."

And when there's any honor that can be got
By pulling strings, he'll get, like as not.

Hiss had been accused of membership in the Communist Party by Whittaker Chambers, whom Alceste Nixon trusted instinctively and identified with: "Although he was a senior editor of *Time* magazine, Chambers was poorly dressed, pudgy, undistinguished in appearance and in background." When Chambers appeared before the committee, the newspaper reporters crowding the congressional hearing room reacted like twentieth-century versions of Versailles courtiers. "Most of the reporters covering the Hiss case were obsessed with style," Alceste wrote. "They were so dazzled by Hiss's background and his brilliant conduct on the witness stand that they failed to see that beneath the unimpressive exterior, Chambers was a stronger, more intelligent man."

The graceful Alger Hiss tripped himself up when Committee Chairman Karl Mundt showed him a photo of Whittaker Chambers and asked him if he had ever known him. At this point, it was simply a matter of one man's word against another's. Hiss could have extricated himself with a charmless *no,* but he made the mistake of showing off.

"If this is a picture of Mr. Chambers," he purred, "he is not particularly unusual looking. He looks like a lot of people. I might even mistake him for the Chairman of this Committee."

Hiss's studied urbanity and supercilious sarcasm got Alceste Nixon's goat: "Hiss's friends from the State Department, other government agencies, and the Washington social community sitting in the front rows of the spectator section broke into a titter of delighted laughter. Hiss acknowledged this reaction to his sally by turning his back on the Committee, tilting his head in a courtly bow, and smiling graciously at his supporters."

> *Notice how tolerant people choose to be*
> *Toward that bold rascal who's at law with me.*
> *His social polish can't conceal his nature;*
> *One sees at once that he's a treacherous creature.*

Still gilding the lily, Hiss asked if Whittaker Chambers were present in the hearing room. "He then looked from side to side, giving the impression that he did not have the slightest idea who this mysterious character might be and that he was anxious to see him in the flesh." Told that Chambers was not present, Hiss assumed a theatrical air of disappointment that roused Alceste Nixon's deepest suspicions.

This artificial style, that's all the fashion,
Has neither taste, nor honesty, nor passion.

"It was a virtuoso performance. . . . But even at that time I was beginning to have some doubts. From considerable experience in observing witnesses on the stand, I had learned that those who are lying or trying to cover up something generally make a common mistake—they tend to overact, to overstate their case. When Hiss had gone through the elaborate show of meticulously examining the photograph of Chambers, and then innocently but also somewhat condescendingly saying that he might even mistake him for the Chairman, he had planted in my mind the first doubt about his credibility."

Alceste Nixon's dogged persistence exposed Hiss. He was jailed for perjury, earning for Alceste the undying hatred of the media courtiers. They hated him relentlessly throughout the eight years he served as vice president, and he hated them in return.

And I despise the frenzied operations
Of all these barterers of protestations,
These lavishers of meaningless embraces,
These utterers of obliging commonplaces. . . .

Alceste Nixon ran for president in 1960 but he lost on looks and style in the first televised debates with John F. Kennedy.

No one could possibly be taken in
By those soft speeches and that sugary grin.
The whole world knows the shady means by which
The low-brow's grown so powerful and rich. . . .
Are you in love with his embroidered hose?
Do you adore his ribbons and his bows?

The answer was yes. Two years later Alceste Nixon ran for governor of California and lost that one too. Calling in the courtiers, he announced that they would no longer have Alceste to kick around.

> *Come then: man's villainy is too much to bear;*
> *Let's leave this jungle and this jackal's lair.*
> *Yes! Treacherous and savage race of men,*
> *You shall not look upon my face again.*

It was his finest hour, but he didn't know it.

Alceste Nixon went into retirement and wrote a political autobiography about the Hiss case and other landmarks of his career called *Six Crises*. As it happened, America had several crises of her own, and so in 1968, Alceste ran for president again.

He was bound to win, considering what had happened to the Democrats. He didn't *have* to try to conceal his real personality but he did it anyway, out of long habit. He came up with the "New Alceste," and devised a campaign slogan promising to "Bring Us Together," making a heroic effort to seem warm and friendly even though it clearly made him uncomfortable. His anomalous cold dark eyes gave off an obsidian flatness that betrayed his scornful opinion of political backslappers.

> *I see you almost hug a man to death,*
> *Exclaim for joy until you're out of breath,*
> *And supplement these loving demonstrations*
> *With endless offers, vows, and protestations. . . .*

His victory sealed his fate. Now that he was president—which is to say, First Nice Guy—he had to go on concealing his real personality. That's when the trouble started. The American electorate, who assuage their own insecurity by demanding Nice Guyism of their leaders, have no idea what years of spurious warmth can do to someone like Alceste Nixon. Nothing is more stressful than a misanthrope trying to be nice with no end in sight. It's hard enough on the people who must witness it, but it just about kills the misanthrope. The strain becomes unbearable; if it goes on too long, paranoia normally kept under control suddenly explodes and the misanthrope starts doing things that he would not ordinarily do.

> *Ah, this is what my sad heart prophesied;*
> *Now all my anxious fears are verified;*
> *My dark suspicion and my gloomy doubt*
> *Divined the truth, and now the truth is out. . . .*
> *Yes, now I have no pity, not a shred;*
> *My temper's out of hand; I've lost my head. . . .*
> *A righteous wrath deprives me of my senses,*
> *And I won't answer for the consequences.*

Alceste Nixon got into some trouble that he could have gotten out of very easily, but he let it go on and build up out of an unconscious need to justify the misanthropy he had denied all his life.

> *I'll discover by this case*
> *Whether or not men are sufficiently base*
> *And impudent and villainous and perverse*
> *To do me wrong before the universe.*

They are.

The "excess of zeal" that set Watergate in motion is the sort of thing that invariably goes on behind a misanthrope's back because a misanthrope's back is usually turned. In a word, we are easy to screw. In *The Palace Guard,* authors Dan Rather and Gary Paul Gates write:

> What gave Haldeman such overwhelming power was that he served as sentinel for a President who chose to sequester himself behind a wall of Do Not Disturb signs. Of all the characteristics that define Richard Nixon, none perhaps is more striking than his celebrated sense of privacy, a trait that he personally attributes to his Quaker heritage.

American loners who would never say "I don't like people" will readily own up to a sense of privacy because it sounds like the Constitution. By attributing his sense of privacy to his Quaker heritage, Nixon got two amendments for the price of one, so to speak. Anyone who objected to it could conceivably be accused of religious bigotry as well as illegal search and seizure.

It might have worked in the nineteenth century, but by the time Nixon appeared on the public scene the Quakers had taken on a quaint, harmless glow like the ruddy, smiling burgher on the oatmeal box. His Quaker-heritage allusion was lost on most Americans, who did not know enough about Quakers to know what they had to do with whatever it was about him that they didn't like. Every time he brought it up, they thought he was just being sanctimonious.

The misanthrope who tries to hide his misanthropy is invariably mistaken for a run-of-the-mill hypocrite and roundly despised. The unabashed misanthrope, on the other hand, evokes a surprising response, as Robert Lewis Taylor notes in his biography of W.C. Fields: "Fields' defiance of civilization, over a period of sixty-seven years, became an institution in which the public took pride. . . . Most persons, as a scholar has noted, harbor a secret affection for anybody with a low opinion of humanity."

This secret affection springs from a universal familiarity with the grind of daily life. For the meek majority who never say what they really think and never get even with the people who do them wrong, the misanthrope is a stand-in whom they can cheer from the safety of the sidelines. He has little to offer victims of crushing evil, but he is the nemesis of humanity's little meannesses, the ones that hurt most of the people most of the time. Engaged in his ceaseless battle against such widespread human failings as officiousness, pomposity, and duplicity, the ostensibly uncharitable misanthrope ironically becomes a warrior for the shat-upon.

A politician could benefit from such a stance, but Nixon would not risk it. A misanthrope is *never* a conformist but Nixon is the exception that proves the rule. His desperate desire to fit in and be accepted is his tragic flaw. Determined to bend himself into the requisite American shape, he spurned the gift of misanthropy bestowed on him by the non-Quaker gods, who punished the indomitable prince of darkness by changing him into a vulnerable Gloomy Gus.

The universal fascination for what-might-have-been is used to clever effect in the vegetable-juice commercial featuring people who gulp down candy bars or ice cream for quick-energy snacks, and then, too late, slap themselves on the forehead and say, "I coulda had a V-8!"

But for our sweet tooth, America coulda had a Richelieu.

Commenting on the only Watergate conspirator who did not break down and confess, Stewart Alsop wrote: "In wartime, G. Gordon Liddy would have been festooned with decorations rather than slapped in jail. As so often in wartime, his stubborn silence did no good."

Liddy disagrees. "I became what I wanted to be," he writes in his autobiography, *Will.* An intimate account of the personal code of honor by which he has chosen to live, the book describes boyhood dreams of Heidelberg dueling scars and German military discipline, grisly tests of courage that included cooking and eating a rat, holding his hand over a flame until his flesh charred, and tying himself to a tree during an electrical storm to "defeat the fear of death and welcome the death of fear."

Statements like this have earned Liddy the tag of psychopath because America has forgotten what "dashing" means. Bursting upon the national scene at the height of the feminist movement, Liddy was dismissed as a comic-machismo anachronism, but in fact he is the spiritual twin of Edmond Rostand's Cyrano de Bergerac: the misanthrope as a stubborn blend of idealist and cynic perfectly balanced in one untroubled soul.

Americans, incapable of understanding that idealism and cynicism always travel in tandem, are forever trying to pry them apart as if they were wheat and chaff. Confronted by a complex personality, we tell ourselves he can't be *this* if he's *that,* but G. Gordon Liddy is most gloriously *this* at the same time he is most gloriously *that,* as he demonstrated when he wrote of Watergate Judge John J. Sirica: "Just as I do, John Sirica believes the end justifies the means. . . . The difference between us is that I admit it openly and don't pretend to be anything other than what I am."

> *I carry my adornments on my soul*
> *I do not dress up like a popinjay;*
> *But inwardly I keep my daintiness. . . .*
> *I go caparisoned in gems unseen,*

Trailing white plumes of freedom, garlanded
With my good name—no figure of a man,
But with a soul clothed in shining armor. . . .

The incredible strength that Liddy showed throughout the seven years of his imprisonment can never be sustained by "love." Only a lordly contempt for the human race and a keen eye for its foibles could have kept him sane, and like Cyrano, he has them in abundance.

Senator Sam Ervin: "Do you swear to tell the truth, the whole truth, and nothing but the truth, so help you God?"

Liddy: "No."

It is my pleasure to displease. I love
Hatred. Imagine how it feels to face
The volley of a thousand angry eyes—
The bile of envy and the froth of fear
Spattering little drops about me. . . .
The Spanish ruff I wear around my throat
Is like a ring of enemies; hard, proud,
Each point another pride, another thorn—
So that I hold myself erect perforce
Wearing the hatred of the common herd
Haughtily, the harsh collar of Old Spain,
At once a fetter and—a halo!

Cyrano was so quick on the uptake that he could write poems while he dueled, *"twirling—thus—a bristling wit,"* his meter keeping time with the cuts of his sword, *"making the sharp truth ring, like golden spurs."*

Liddy on Charles Colson's conversion: "If he'd run over his grandmother for Nixon, imagine what he'll do for Jesus."

Liddy lighting his cigar on a peace marcher's candle: "There, you useless son of a bitch. At least now you've been good for something."

Nowadays, Liddy's brand of antiquated honor exists only in jails. Of his fellow inmates he wrote: "Do them a favor or an injury, honor requires them to repay it, and they were constantly looking for some way to do so." The respectable majority is terrified of cavalier panache, but the inmates of Danbury Prison idolized Liddy when he used Watergate methods to expose corrupt wardens. Black prisoners especially respected him because they instinctively understood and identified with his refusal to give in and cooperate with the government like the other Watergate figures.

> *What would you have me do?*
> *Seek for the patronage of some great man,*
> *And like a creeping vine on a tall tree*
> *Crawl upward, where I cannot stand alone?*
> *No thank you!*
> *Be a buffoon in the vile hope of teasing a smile*
> *On some cold face? No thank you!*
> *Make my knees callous, and cultivate a supple spine,*
> *Wear out my belly groveling in the dust?*
> *No thank you!*

Liddy's idealism and cynicism are still going strong. In an appearance last year on the Howard Stern radio talk show, he described George Bush as "a man who can't keep his word," and punctiliously refused to answer questions that verged even slightly on legal opinions because: "I was disbarred. I want you to understand that."

Yet during a "Crossfire" debate about the Iran-Contra hearings, he pointed out dryly that no one should be surprised that Oliver North shredded documents because the government issued him a shredding machine, and what else did they expect him to do with it?

TOURETTE'S
MISANTHROPY

The *New York Times* reviewer of *Lump It or Leave It* said that I reminded her of "someone with Tourette's syndrome at a diplomats' ball."

Tourette's Misanthropy is idealism with a short fuse. Its earliest known sufferer was Coriolanus, the patrician general and failed politician of Republican Rome.

The character of Coriolanus in Shakespeare's play has been called a "splendid oaf." A Patton in spirit but lacking Patton's intellectual streak, the Shakespearean Coriolanus is a consummate aristocrat within the original Old Roman definition: honor incorruptible and consumption so inconspicuous that you can't tell by looking whether he is rich or not. As the puzzled senators say of him, "He covets less than misery itself would give."

It goes without saying that Coriolanus would make a great statesman, but in order to be elected consul on the patrician ticket he must first become a great politician. His friend and campaign manager, Menenius, assesses his candidate's chances.

His nature is too noble for the world:
He would not flatter Neptune for his trident,
Or Jove for his power to thunder.
His heart's his mouth:
What his breast forges, that his tongue must vent.

Menenius tries to impress upon his candidate the importance of wooing the plebeians but Coriolanus recoils. He hates the common people and thinks God made far too many of them. Entering the Forum for his first campaign speech, he greets the assembled plebeians in his own inimitable fashion.

What's the matter, you dissentious rogues,
That, rubbing the poor itch of your opinion,
Make yourselves scabs?
Who deserves greatness
Deserves your hate; and your affections are
A sick man's appetite. . . .
He that depends upon your favours swims
With fins of lead. . . .

Menenius, a born spin doctor, whispers urgently, "This is the way to kindle, not to quench." But Coriolanus, cranked up and really into it by now, ignores him and launches into his plan for solving the famine problem.

Would the nobility lay aside their ruth
And let me use my sword, I'd make a quarry
With thousands of these quartered slaves,
As high as I could pick my lance.

When the mob starts howling in protest, Coriolanus calls them a "musty superfluity" and bellows, "Oh, go home, you fragments!"

Menenius calls a damage-control confab and puts out the word that Coriolanus's "noble carelessness" often makes him speak roughly, but in his heart he really loves the common people and has proved it many times by his heroic service in the army. He has twenty-seven war wounds, Menenius points out—"every gash an enemy's grave"—and promises that Coriolanus will go to the Forum in a toga of humility and show his wounds to the people.

Coriolanus balks at the idea but Menenius convinces him that it's an excellent way to show his human side. Coriolanus reluctantly agrees, so off they go to the Forum to put a spin on his first disastrous outing.

It might have worked if Coriolanus had told the plebeians a few war stories first and built up gradually to the subject of his wounds, but instead he immediately rips open his toga of humility and yells:

> *Look, sir, my wounds!*
> *I got them in my country's service, when*
> *Some certain of your brethren roared and ran*
> *From the noise of our own drums.*

"O me, the gods!" Menenius groans. "You must not speak of that: you must desire them to think upon you."

"Hang 'em!" Coriolanus replies, not troubling to lower his voice.

"Pray speak to them in wholesome manner," Menenius begs.

"Bid them wash their faces, and keep their teeth clean."

Next, Coriolanus tells the mob point-blank that he wants their votes.

First Citizen: "The price is, to ask it kindly."

Third Citizen: "You have not loved the common people."

Coriolanus: "You should account me the more virtuous, that I have not been common in my love."

As the heckling mounts, Coriolanus loses what little patience he has and yells, "Why in this wolfish toga should I stand here to beg of Hob and Dick?"

The tribunes denounce him as an enemy of the people and demand his banishment. Menenius and Coriolanus's womenfolk beg him to go to the Forum and answer the charges against him.

"You have been too rough. You must return and mend it."

But he still doesn't get it. "Why did you wish me milder?" he asks. "Would you have me false to my nature? Rather say, I play the man I am."

Surrounded by pragmatists, he finally agrees to try and mend his fences once more. "Well, I must do it: Away, my disposition, and possess me some harlot's spirit! I will answer in mine honour."

"Ay, but mildly," Menenius cautions.

"Well, mildly be it, then,—mildly!"

Smoldering all the way to the Forum, by the time he gets there he is so worked up that he explodes at the mere sight of the expectant plebeians, whose value to the state he analyzes in another extemporaneous speech.

> *Mutable, rank-scented mob!*
> *In soothing them, we nourish against our senate*
> *The cockle of rebellion, insolence, sedition,*
> *Which we ourselves have ploughed for*
> *By mingling them with us.*

He calls the plebeians "measles" and their tribune a "Triton of the minnows." When an old man tries to take hold of his arm, he pushes him off, barking, "Hence, rotten thing! or I shall shake thy bones out of thy garments!"

A riot breaks out. Enter the aediles (cops) but the situation is now beyond control. When the tribunes accuse Coriolanus of seeking tyrannical power and urge the plebeians to kill him, he draws his sword and offers to take on the whole crowd.

> *The fires in the lowest hell fold in the people!*
> *You common cry of curs whose breath I hate!*
> *Whose loves I prize*
> *As the dead carcasses of unburied men*
> *That do corrupt my air,—I banish you!*

Infuriated by the slurs on his honor and the compromises he has been forced to make, Coriolanus suddenly compromises himself. Blind to the irony of his action, he decides to avenge his honor by committing treason. He goes over to the enemy, the Volscians, and offers to help them invade Rome, his "cankered country," promising to fight "with the spleen of all the under fiends" of hell. He would rather ally himself with his old adversary, the Volscian general Aufidius, whom he once called "a lion I am proud to hunt," than let his principles be trampled by the Roman mob.

His wife and mother go to the enemy camp to dissuade him. Their pleas are so heartrending that Coriolanus gives in and agrees to return to Rome. But it's too late: now he is a traitor to the Volscians, and their leader Aufidius is not the honorable man Coriolanus has judged him to be. He is subject to peer pressure— "Our virtues lie in the interpretation of the time"—so when the

Volscians demand the death of Coriolanus, Aufidius orders his execution.

When I first read *Coriolanus* in college we had a vigorous classroom discussion about his decision to commit treason. My classmates were either shocked or puzzled by his act but I was neither. I identified thoroughly with him but I kept quiet because my reason was too complicated to explain, and if I had attempted to do so, everybody would have laughed because it involved walnuts.

It happened on Christmas Day, 1940. I was four. Preparing for a day of company, my grandmother gave me a bowl of walnuts in the shell and told me to put them on the coffee table. I carried them successfully through the kitchen, but when I was halfway across the living room, three or four walnuts spilled out of the bowl onto the floor.

There really is something to the expression, "I was so mad I couldn't see straight." Outlines and edges of things shifted momentarily like pictures coming out of their frames. The next thing I knew, I had turned the bowl upside down and dumped all the walnuts on the floor in a deafening tattoo.

My grandmother had seen it. "What in the world did you do that for?"

"If I spill a few, I'm going to spill them all," I said grimly.

Then, my fury expended, I very calmly picked up the walnuts, taking care to get every one, replaced them in the bowl, and put it on the table as directed.

When I told this story to a psychiatrist twenty-five years later, she immediately jumped to the conclusion that I had panicked over failing to meet my grandmother's perfectionist standards of Southern elegance. That's what you get for talking to psychiatrists: they are the master mold of conventional thinking and the very glass of superficiality. My "perfectionist" grandmother's housekeeping was predicated on the hearty Anglo-Saxon maxim, "A little dirt never hurt anybody"; she would not have cared if I had picked *shelled* walnuts off the floor and put them back in the bowl. As for elegance, the reason the walnuts made a deafening tattoo was that we had linoleum instead of rugs.

The walnut incident was my first episode of Tourette's Misanthropy: idealism with a short fuse. There have been many others since. The most recent one was as fraught with irony as Coriolanus's decision to compromise himself to keep from being compromised and dishonor himself to keep from being dishonored. As far as anyone in the publishing world knows—and just about everyone in the publishing world has now heard this story—I did what no writer has ever done before: raised hell about a favorable review.

I say *favorable* because the reviewer said nice things about *Reflections in a Jaundiced Eye*. It was not, however, a *good* review because it broke just about every rule of the reviewing art—and reviewing *is* an art, which is why I went ballistic. I cherish the review-as-literature; as lapidary journalism in the eighteenth-century mode, the last hard sparkling diamond in the essayist's tarnished crown. To me, writing a good review is not just a way to make extra money, but a sacred duty.

As soon as I read the review of *Eye* I wanted to shoot the reviewer, but since I couldn't do that, I did the next best thing and wrote him a letter. It said, in part:

You do not know how to write a review. I do. Here are your faults:

1. A book review is a news story about a book and should carry a short, tight lead with a reader hook. Your Tarleton twins lead rambles on forever and goes nowhere. I told this story in the book

to make a point—that I hate children and hence was quite pleased when Granny told me I had eaten one—but you simply tell it without ever making the point about children, or any point at all. When you finally stop talking about the Tarleton twins, you leave the reader with the idea that the book is about Southern women, which it is not.

2. You wrote: "As she says of the Wall Street guy who skipped the sex scenes in a novel about money, 'I want to get to the good parts.' " In the first place, this is a sliding attribution resulting from a careless reading of the passage. It was the Wall Street guy, not me, who said "I want to get to the good parts." Then in your next sentence you say: "That's what this new book of essays is about. The good parts." This implies that my book is about money, which is one of the few things it *isn't* about.

3. Your description of men as "once chaotic and Heathcliff-like" bears no resemblance to the old-fashioned manly virtues that I praise in the book. You paraphrased something I never said, and you did it with a particularly unthought-out and meaningless choice of words. When were men as a group ever "chaotic?" Were you trying to say dashing, gallant, courageous, daring, devil-may-care? I've known plenty of chaotic women but no chaotic men until I read your review.

4. You don't have an eye and an ear for the telling quote. If you hadn't quoted the shaft I gave Mary Gordon, no one reading your review would have any idea of the tone of my book. Yet by choosing to quote what I said about Gordon, you made things hard on yourself and took up valuable space because you had to quote her twice before my shaft would make any sense. With all the quotable one-liners in my book that can stand alone, why did you decide to get tangled up in that one?

5. You concentrated on too many minor points and in general farted around without ever stating fully the two things that must

be in every review: what the book is about, and what the reviewer thinks of it.

    6. When reviewing a volume of discrete essays such as this one, the reviewer must identify and state the central theme that links them all together. You go from a hokey "She's not real pleased with things" to a quick reference to Alexander Hamilton which you promptly drop. Of the reviews I've had so far, the best statement of theme comes from the *Washington Times:* "Miss King is a fussy old maid who doesn't suffer fools and likes to see fools suffer."

I sent a copy of this letter to the book section editor, and then wrote her a letter saying that her method of choosing reviewers (I maintain that she tries to match reviewer and author too closely by genre and region, something we had argued about before) had produced one "who used my navel for his navel gazing."

According to a New York acquaintance of mine who heard a discussion of this episode at a literary cocktail party, the considered opinion of all present was that I'm crazy.

If I am, so is Carlton Fisk.

The forty-three-year-old Chicago White Sox catcher is a jovial, well-liked man, but he is an old-fashioned New Englander with rigid standards about how and how not to play baseball. Early in the 1990 season, Fisk did something without precedent in the major leagues: he blew his stack and chewed out a player on the opposing team for making a mistake.

The White Sox were playing the Yankees in New York. During the Yankee half of the inning, twenty-two-year-old "Neon" Deion Sanders, so called because of the flashy gold chains he wears on the field, hit an easy pop-up. Assuming it would be caught, Sanders strolled toward first base, then turned and ambled nonchalantly back to the Yankee dugout before the fielder had the ball in his glove.

Suddenly, looming behind him, was the six-foot-two Fisk, bellowing like a bull.

"Run it out, you piece of crud! Go on, run it out!"

Sanders stared at him in disbelief, obviously thinking that he must have lost his mind. He clearly had no idea why Fisk was incensed but he found out the next time he came to bat.

The huge catcher rose from his squat and gave him a murderous look.

"The days of slavery are over," said Sanders, who is black.

"Let me tell you something, you little [epithet not printed in the newspaper]," said Fisk. "There is a right way and a wrong way to play this game. You're playing it the wrong way. And the rest of us don't like it. Someday you're going to get this game shoved right down your throat."

Naturally both benches cleared—something that never happens, unfortunately, in the publishing world. Afterwards Fisk explained why he had castigated Sanders. He did it, he said, for "truth, justice, and the American way, and to keep Lou Gehrig from spinning in his grave."

Washington Post sportswriter Thomas Boswell understood Fisk's violent reaction and wrote a moving tribute to him.

Call it the last stand of the dinosaurs. We may never see the like again, in any pro sport. So relish it. . . .

Fisk is profoundly anachronistic and proud of it. He's out of step with the times. . . . Perhaps what sets Fisk apart is his antiquated notion that baseball is a calling, not just a silly game. Like a soldier, a cop, a priest, he reveres his forebears and is delighted to think he's worthy of them. What was good enough for Rogers Hornsby and Willie Mays is good enough for him.

Fisk is an idealist with a short fuse who suffers from Tourette's Misanthropy.

Another sufferer, who may well be the reincarnation of Coriolanus, is John Silber, the Democrat who lost the Massachusetts governor's race because his heart is his mouth. "Silber's shockers," as his brusque remarks were called, turned every liberal in America into a spin doctor and had Ellen Goodman agonizing for weeks: should she, could she, vote for a *Republican* to keep the mean-spirited Coriolanus from solving the social problems without which she would have nothing to write about? Her last column before the election ended on a note that was straight out of "The Lady—or the Tiger?" but her deft touch with suspense is about as deft as all her other touches. It was pretty clear that she voted for the palely loitering Wasp.

The prickly, unashamedly elitist Gore Vidal, if not an actual misanthrope, shows great promise. A gentleman of the old school despite such lapses as *Myra Breckinridge,* Vidal definitely has Tourette's Misanthropy on the subject of America's growing egalitarian inclination to deny the existence of inborn talent.

"This is the American attitude," he told *Publishers Weekly.* "Anybody can bull through it, or fake it. Faking it is our great national pastime. They always think that if you write well you're somehow cheating, you're not being democratic by writing as badly as everybody else does."

America's readiness to hurl a charge of elitism at anyone who insists that things be done well puts victims of Tourette's Misanthropy at daily risk of death from a sudden, massive stroke. I thought I was a goner when I read the following letter to the *Washington Post* from one George Wooley.

The many books on "correct" grammar are merely helpful guides to better communication skills. Who decides what grammar rules or spelling are officially correct? It's not set in stone. New words and phrases and new uses for old words and phrases are part of the art of language and the art must not be stifled by a few scholarly decisions.

The sole purpose of any communication, written or oral, is to convey a message, and it is far more important that the message delivered is correctly interpreted than it is that the message is in a "correct" form.

The eye stumbles over that last clause, which should read: *it is far more important that the message delivered be correctly interpreted than that it be in a "correct" form.* But never mind that. Let's make this egalitarian twit run out his pop fly.

In 1327, King Edward II of England was deposed and imprisoned in Berkeley Castle. Three goons hired by the rebellious Welsh barons were standing by to murder him, but they were afraid to act without the protection of written orders from Queen Isabel's chief henchman, a bishop who was in on the plot.

The bishop was equally afraid to put anything in writing. If something went wrong and the queen needed a fall guy, he did not want an execution order in his handwriting floating around. He needed an escape hatch; he had to figure out some way to make his message equivocal enough so that he could claim it was an order of reprieve *or* an order of execution, whichever the situation called for.

What to do?

Taking a leaf from today's anti-elitists, the bishop decided that it was far more important that his message be correctly interpreted than that it be in correct form, so he composed a sentence in which he intentionally omitted a vital comma. The sentence was: *Kill Edward not to fear is good.*

Depending upon where they chose to "see" the comma, the

goons could read it as: *Kill Edward not, to fear is good.* Or they could read it as: *Kill Edward, not to fear is good.* Knowing what they were supposed to do, they chose the second version. But for a comma, regicide was done and all the conspirators were covered.

If you feel like screaming, tearing your hair, and rending your garments over ignorance, incompetence, semiliteracy, and the curious pride so many Americans take in all three, you have Tourette's Misanthropy.

If you want to take slothful, rude, careless, unpunctual people by the lapels and shake them until their teeth rattle, you have Tourette's Misanthropy.

If you get the urge to kill when you hear plangent elegies about "babies having babies" in the inner cities, and then open a woman's magazine to find an interview with a famous movie star about the joys of her unwed motherhood, you have Tourette's Misanthropy.

If you spend the evening snapping and snarling at your spouse because your newspaper contains an op-ed calling Martin Luther King's plagiarism "textual appropriation" and "voice merging," you have Tourette's Misanthropy.

Don't worry about it, don't feel guilty about it, and for God's sake don't waste your money on a psychiatrist to find out what's wrong with you, because there is nothing wrong with you. Remember, *you* are right, and *they* are wrong. If you start feeling depressed, do what I do and recite Cyrano de Bergerac's farewell.

> *Yes, all my laurels you have riven away*
> *And all my roses; yet in spite of you,*
> *There is one crown I bear away with me,*
> *And tonight, when I enter before God,*

WITH CHARITY TOWARD NONE

My salute shall sweep all the stars away
From the blue threshold. One thing without stain,
Unspotted from the world, in spite of doom
Mine own—my white plume.

MS.-ANTHROPES

"Female misanthrope" is an oxymoron. Women are philanthro-
pists in the original sense of the word, before money got involved
in it. Despite a quarter century of feminism, people who deal
with female raw emotions, from counselors of battered wives to
teachers of karate, report that women still say, "I can't get angry
enough."

One would expect more women to become misanthropic now
that they are hardly ever alone. At least the traditional housewife
of the feminine-mystique era had the house to herself for a few
hours each day, but today's beset Having It Alls lack even that.
Yet when women talk about "privacy" they mean abortion
rights, and the millions of words feminists have written about "a
room of one's own" refer to psychological space, rarely to physical solitude. For most women, being alone is tantamount to
being deserted.

Women meet hatred with salvos of bigger and better niceness

98

and warnings of "There's more niceness where that came from." However much you pretty it up, this is masochism, and no misanthrope was ever a masochist. The opposite, it must be confessed, is more likely to be the case. My own sadism is the psychological kind known as "gleeful," rather than the physical kind, but both are distinctly unfeminine.

The ranks of distaff misanthropy are therefore thin, but one shining exception has walked this earth, and she makes me look like Little Bo Peep.

A six-foot-one, gun-toting virago whose sobriquet was "the gorilla lady" was not a woman to cross, but somebody finally did. On December 27, 1985, Dian Fossey was butchered at the Karisoke Centre for Mountain Gorilla Research in Rwanda where she had spent eighteen tumultuous years.

She was found in bed, her head split in two by a machete left nearby. Half-empty bottles of beer and scotch sat on her worktable beside an unloaded pistol. The murderer had entered her cabin through a hole cut out of the tin wall. The most puzzling aspect of the macabre scene was the hair clutched in her stiff hands: it was her own.

Solving Fossey's murder was not the purpose of the late Harold Hayes, who died in 1989 just as he was completing his engrossing biography, *The Dark Romance of Dian Fossey*. Whodunit interests him less than whydunit, and here he hits pay dirt, for there were very few people in Dian Fossey's embattled life who did *not* have a motive for murdering her.

> Poachers, cattle herders, park officials, Western conservationists, members of her staff, a couple dozen researchers—the parade of possible suspects extended far back into the past. . . . Fossey had shot at her enemies, kidnapped their children, whipped them about the genitals, smeared them with ape dung, killed their

cattle, burned their property, and sent them to jail. Anyone who dared to threaten her gorillas, or even to challenge her methods, set her off, and the force of her malevolence was difficult to imagine.

Born in the Bay Area in 1932, Fossey attended San Jose State College. Drawn to children, especially helpless ones, she became a physical therapist at a Louisville, Kentucky hospital. Refusing to live in nursing quarters, she insisted on renting a remote cabin deep in the woods miles outside of town. The landlord, who had advertised the place for a couple, refused at first to rent it to her, saying it was too isolated for a woman alone and he would not be responsible for her safety. She threatened to return to California if she could not have the cabin, so her supervisor at the hospital called the landlord and explained that Fossey's position had been hard to fill and they could not risk losing her.

The landlord relented and Fossey moved into the cottage, where she lived alone for ten years, collecting stray dogs instead of boyfriends. Eventually she moved to an even more remote house when she returned from a vacation and found that the landlord had put a mobile home for his aunts too near her place.

The consensus among her co-workers was that she liked animals better than people. When they gathered for coffee, she refused to join them and took her breaks alone. In what was probably a subconscious decision to insure that others kept their distance, she was less than fastidious in her grooming and often gave off body odor.

A fervent desire to see exotic animals led her to borrow $8,000 to go to Africa. It was on this trip that her enormous ego first reared its head and gave hints of megalomaniacal excesses to come. Completely flat-chested, wheezing with emphysema from her three-pack-a-day habit, and often smelly from not bathing, she nonetheless thought every man she met was trying to seduce her, and hurled accusations of sexual harassment when they did not respond to her up-front offers.

Hiring the last of the Great White Hunters, John Alexander, to take her on private safari, she laid it on the line: "What makes you think sex has anything to do with love? Here we've been three weeks on safari. We could have shacked up together and had a hell of a good time." When Alexander modestly declined, she spread the story that he was "all over me all the time."

Her articles on the trip (and the accompanying photos that she "borrowed" from a more experienced photographer and neglected to credit) attracted the attention of the famous prehistorian Louis Leakey, who preferred female assistants for his ape studies because "women were more patient, more sensitive to mother-infant relations, and less likely to arouse aggression in males." Little did he know that his latest Galatea would nearly start a civil war.

Arriving in East Africa in the sixties "when just to be white was to risk your life," Fossey's Tugboat-Annie nerve became an advantage in the face of Communist-inspired Simba incursions. Much of what happened in East Africa at this time was not reported by a press eager to put a good face on newly emerging nations, but Hayes fills in the blanks with some riveting passages:

> Led by witch doctors, the Simbas believed themselves impervious to bullets. They stoked their courage on hashish, and dressed themselves in monkey skins and whatever else might be at hand— lamp shades, women's panties, chicken feathers. . . . Many [of their victims] died by being forced to drink gasoline, then their stomachs were cut open and set on fire. One specially prized victim, a moderate politician named Sylvere Bondekwe, saw his liver cut out and eaten while he was still alive. . . . In their

extended siege of Stanleyville years earlier, the Simbas had held 1,100 Belgians and Americans hostage. "We shall cut out the hearts of the Americans and Belgians and wear them as fetishes," the Simbas had announced. "We shall dress ourselves in the skins of the Americans and Belgians."

Joseph Mobutu, financed by the United States for his anti-Communist resistance, swore to put down the Simbas. Knowing the limitations of his own army—"In a crisis, Congolese soldiers tended to drop their guns, take off their shoes, and run"—he hired white soldiers of fortune to protect his own position. When the white mercenaries, many of whom held Nazi-style racial views, turned against Mobutu and began killing their black comrades-in-arms, Mobutu announced that Europeans were trying to take over the country and ordered all whites killed.

It was at this time that Fossey claimed she was held for two days in a cage and "raped and raped and raped" by black African soldiers. No one knows what actually happened. One story has it that she was urinated on and otherwise humiliated, but that she escaped actual rape by defying her tormentors with the force of her rage, screaming, "You don't have the balls to rape me!"

It has the ring of truth, given Fossey's hell-for-leather personality, and it might have worked for a woman over six feet tall. Leakey believed her rape story, but the son of Congo colonialists did not: "If any African raped a European in that part of the world," he told the author, "you might as well forget that European's existence. . . . You don't get out of those kinds of camps."

This same ex-colonialist, on discovering that Fossey intended to stay and study gorillas come hell or high water, gave her some practical advice:

"The only option you've got to stay alive is to make yourself into some sort of spiritual witch. You've got to do this with such effectiveness and create such a sense of terror about you, people will give you a wide berth. All over Africa, there have been European women who lived on farms by themselves while their husbands went to war—my mother was one of them. The only way they survived was to become known as some sort of banshee. All Africans, you know, live in a spook land. They believe almost everything is invested with spiritual meaning. . . . I suggested she should make herself into someone no one would want to go *near*—that she should get wailing systems, smoke bombs, false faces, that sort of thing.

"At the same time, I told her she should beat the bejesus out of anybody she felt like beating the bejesus out of. And then they would get the feeling there was a woman up there who was behaving totally unwomanly."

This is precisely what Fossey did. To stop farmers from grazing their herds on the gorilla preserve, she shot a cow and vowed to shoot one a month: the grazing stopped. When farmers kidnapped her dog, she kidnapped eight of their cattle and spread the word that she would shoot one cow a day until she got her dog back: she got it back by nightfall. Abandoning her gorilla work to track the killers of a water buffalo, she fired a clip at them. Spotting one of their children hiding behind a tree, she kidnapped the child and offered to exchange him for his father's spear: she got the spear. "Naturally I returned the brat," she wrote to Leakey.

Word of her incredible courage began to spread. The Africans had never seen a woman like Fossey:

In a country where women were subservient to men, this giant female *mzungu* [European]—looming over the pint-sized Hutu and Batwa—was subservient to no one. . . . So effective were her techniques of terrorizing the Africans that some members of her staff believed she had supernatural powers. One day, a tracker brought the body of a small child into her camp. He asked her to cure it, to bring the child back to life. He had no doubt that the white witch could do this.

Rwanda became her only home. After her affair with Robert Campbell ended in 1972 she sloughed off the few friendships she had ever made back in America and burned the bridges connecting her to her life in her native land. She endured the occasional company of the embassy people, who had to endure hers for political reasons even though she called the wife of one official a cunt.

The "Malthusian nightmare" of densely populated Rwanda drove her to fury as she watched the native peoples overwhelm the preserve, their only source of food and water, crowding her beloved gorillas out of existence. In an extreme reaction to the encroachment of her own species, Fossey became a surrogate mother to infant gorillas, "tending them night and day as though they were her own babies, feeding them, cuddling them, sleeping with them in her cabin, covered with their diarrhea."

She flew into a rage if people interrupted her work. When a group of Chicago tourists showed up unannounced, she fired bullets over their heads and sent them scrambling back down the mountain in fear of their lives. Her own scientific staff felt her iron hand. "The person who runs a field station sets its style. Fossey's was hermitic. She stayed in her cabin all day and all night, and expected the researchers to stay in theirs when they weren't in the field. They all ate their meals alone. If they wanted to say something to somebody, they sent a note."

A National Geographic producer saw her beat four African

porters with her walking stick. Another saw her threaten a cap-
tured poacher with castration. "She would approach the
poacher, holding pliers or machete, looking at that part of their
anatomy. . . . All during the brutal ritual, Fossey shouted ob-
scenities at the prisoner, a mixture of words that came into her
head—English, French, German, Swahili, communicating a feeling of absolute outrage."

State Department cables flew when she asked the Rwandan
government for permission to kill poachers on sight. "It is now
only a matter for the President to give the order—KILL—[be-
cause] the prisons are already over-crowded and this is the only
way we are going to be able to protect the remaining gorillas,"
she announced.

But somebody killed her first. She was buried in the gorilla
graveyard she started when her special pet, Digit, was killed by
poachers. The Rwandan government tried and convicted her
African tracker, who allegedly committed suicide in his cell. Her
American assistant Wayne McGuire, whom she had bawled out
two days before her death, was also convicted in absentia after
he returned to the United States, but Rwanda has never tried to
extradite him.

I found it interesting that the other reviewers of this book
stopped short of calling Fossey a misanthrope. Most concluded
that she had "gone bushy"—the African version of cabin fever—
which could be construed as another way of saying "better insane than unfriendly." Others, especially female reviewers, said
that her ostensible hatred of people proved that she really "hated
herself"—a favorite American rationalization for misanthropy.

They either missed or chose to ignore a passage in the book
indicating that gorilla ladies do things differently. Speaking on
condition of anonymity, another female primatologist told the
author: "I didn't like humans. The monkeys allowed me to opt

out, to get my need for social interaction and social closeness, so I didn't have to pay the price of human interaction."

So it was with Dian Fossey, a blip on the radar screen of Smile Button America. I suspect that citizenship in the Republic of Nice had a great deal to do with her behavior. In other countries, congenital introverts simply remain introverts all their lives, neither advancing nor retreating, but America's commitment to extroversion as a national art form can abrade some naturally aloof personalities until they flower into deadly nightshade.

Children are admirably gimlet-eyed before adults put them through the American make-over program. When *Snow White and the Seven Dwarfs* came out in 1940, my favorite dwarf was Grumpy, and for once I conformed: Grumpy was the overwhelming favorite of children, and Grumpy dolls outsold all the others. (As children of the Depression we had to choose *one* doll; today's children would get the whole set and this valuable statistic would be unavailable.)

Unfortunately, something happens to change most children from baleful realists to peepulphiles, and that something is school. "Much may be made of a Scotchman if he be caught young," said Samuel Johnson, and he was right.

As the enforced extroversion and other-directedness of school closed in on me, I felt compelled to remain Scotch, as it were. I invented a game called "making it night": closing the blinds and curtains and turning on all the lights during the day. It was, I know now, my way of banishing the Little Mary Sunshine that school, my first American institution, expected me to be. As I got older, I developed a love of rain and cold weather as other symbols of solitude, and instinctively distrusted anyone whose favorite season was summer.

I can identify with Dian Fossey shrouded in the mists of her mountain aerie, but her fixation on that isolated Kentucky cabin and what she went through to get it tell me more about her than any of her African experiences.

I know the panic she must have felt when the landlord refused to rent it to her. I know the blind rage she must have felt when she threatened to quit her new job if she could not live alone. I know the emotional exhaustion she must have undergone when she had to run around making phone calls and explaining herself to people so they would intercede for her. I know the crumple of relief she must have felt when she got the cabin after all. And I know the shame that surely came over her when involuntary gratitude crept into the relief and she found herself saying "thank you" to the landlord for letting her be a loner.

That cabin—and those coffee breaks—are all I need to know to understand why she ended up in Africa beating the bejesus out of anybody who got in her way.

That Dian Fossey was a Mean Green is indisputable. She was as wacky and brutal as today's battlers against "speciesism" who believe in civil rights for spotted owls, but the resemblance ends there. Ready and willing to go it alone, she committed all her outrages without the help of screaming minions on college break. Unlike the tree spikers of Oregon, there was nothing sneaky about her, and she had guts.

In an America drowning in Happy Talk, a woman who refused a rabies vaccine with "I'm no more rabid than usual" has my undying admiration.

Female misanthropes in literature are even rarer than in life, but I found one.

The Prodigal Women, written by Nancy Hale, edited by Max Perkins, published in 1942, is my "desert island book," the one I would want with me if I were shipwrecked and had to read the same book over and over—and I've already read it twenty times.

Set in Boston in the 1920s, its theme is: "People who need people are the unluckiest people in the world."

Leda March, the protagonist, is the bookish daughter of an unimportant branch of a rich Brahmin family. She's happy moping about the woods, hating girls with school spirit and being hated by them, but suddenly she acquires a best girlfriend.

Betsy Jekyll, a Southern transplant who prides herself on her Jazz Age "pep," overwhelms Leda with puppydog friendliness and drags her home to meet the frantically hospitable Jekyll family who have just moved North.

Mother Jekyll would rather fill her house than clean it. Rolling back the rugs and playing the piano for her dancing daughters, screaming "Stay for supper!" over the din, she exudes gregariousness. The older daughter Maizie, the family beauty, is a Southern belle knee-deep in popularity and hysterical gaiety. Chattering a mile a minute, tossing dresses aside, spilling perfume, she puts on a theater of femininity for the rapt Leda and Betsy who gather in her room to watch her dress.

Leda loves all this—yet she doesn't. She senses that the Jekyll women would die without people to validate their existence, and she doesn't want to be that way. She longs to flee from them and the emotional dependency they represent.

Leda turns into a beauty and comes to the attention of her socially powerful aunt who sponsors her debutante year. Her sudden entrée into the top drawer of society gives her a perfect excuse to drop the emotionally threatening Jekylls, who are déclassé, and so she does.

She becomes the toast of the season—with an ironic twist. Rid of the Jekylls' encroachment on her inner space, she must now cope with all of Boston. Savoring her power over the girls who used to make fun of her, she puts herself on automatic pilot and plunges into the social fray, becoming the debutante who never sleeps.

When her handsome older cousin James begs her to marry him, her triumph is complete. She is now in a position to recoup the place in society her dowdy parents lost. With her looks and James's money she can be Boston's leading hostess and most sought-after young matron. . . . except that she doesn't like people.

What she really wants to be is a Boston bluestocking.

[It] was inconceivable to her that people, human beings, could ever awaken the kind of hesitant tenderness, the warmth, that came to her when she read great words, or when words formed themselves in her imagination. . . . Her life would be pure, and severe; spent in learning, absorbing. Her life would be as white as alabaster, never smeared with the soil that came from living minds. . . . she imagined her room, the room where she would study all the days. . . . the thousands of books, the millions of books. . . .

While Leda dreams of sensible shoes, the Jekyll sisters pursue ultrafeminine destinies. Betsy, a monster of other-directedness, goes to New York and becomes the consummate Flapper. Scatty Maizie falls in love with Boston scion-turned-painter Lambert Rudd, an inner-directed creator who puts his work first and needs nothing from people. Virile but wary, he wants an emotionally self-sufficient woman who will leave him alone to paint.

Threatened by Lambert's detachment, Maizie hurls herself against him like a wave at a rock. "He was a hundred worlds away from her, talking about his work. . . . All of her nature was gathered, drawn up in a knot, wanting him and seeking about for a means of getting him. . . . [She was] goaded to desperation by his remoteness, by her impotence to engage him."

She gets pregnant and refuses to have an abortion, so he reluctantly marries her. On their extended honeymoon in South America, Lambert is so morose and distant that the insecure Maizie, desperate to please him, aborts the baby after all and develops a gynecological infection. The trip, which was supposed to give Lambert a chance to paint, turns into a mobile medical unit and Lambert turns into a nurse. Waiting on her, keeping track of her medicines, he can no longer concentrate on his painting and begins to loathe her for "the base hurly-burly that his mind had become."

The inner-directed Lambert and the inner-directed Leda meet and fall in love, but Maizie goes to pieces when Lambert asks her for a divorce. The ensuing uproar is too much for Leda's pristine temperament; "she did not want to be so near to people as that. . . . she had stuck her head into a nest of passion."

She marries the dull, adoring James and salvages her emotional detachment by transmuting it into the society matron's brittleness. Lambert is not so lucky; his emotional detachment is shattered by Maizie's invalidism. Becoming pregnant again, she takes to her bed and stays there to guard against miscarriage. Knowing that his gruffness makes her hysterical, Lambert learns to hide it. "He said everything very softly, smiled cautiously, hoping that he wouldn't get her all upset." Eventually all spontaneity in him is stifled, and with it his artistic talent.

Maizie is happy and calm during her pregnancy, but once the baby is born her old insecurity returns. Now that she's well, Lambert will stop waiting on her, stop speaking softly, stop smiling warmly. Haunted by the specter of his renewed detachment, she has a Grand Guignol nervous breakdown as only a

Southern belle can, complete with auditory and visual hallucinations.

After Maizie enters an asylum, Lambert has an affair with the now-divorced Leda. Because each grants the other his own space, his artistic talent reawakens and she begins writing poetry. Soon their idyll is interrupted by Maizie's psychiatrist, who pronounces her well enough to live on the outside with her husband and daughter. Lambert's cooperation being vital to her full recovery, he goes to live with her in a house in the hospital town. Reluctantly, because Lambert asks her to, Leda takes a country house nearby so they can continue seeing each other.

But Maizie finds out about it and goes to pieces again. Repelled by this spectacle of intimacy turned to cannibalism, and realizing what Lambert's surrender to the world of people has done to him, Leda spurns him and admits to herself that she is a misanthrope.

"My spiritual home . . . my way of life is alone. It always was. I always knew it." Solitude wins, and with it her old dream of writing. "Creation lives alone in a small temple. Only one may worship at a time. That was my gift at birth, that was all I ever had. I was given the private means of purification." She walks off through the woods she loved as a girl, resolving "to live alone, without desire. . . . All sin lies in the life of people, all virtue for me alone."

I don't know how the women's studies crowd has managed to miss *The Prodigal Women* in their eternal quest for the literature of "autonomy." If Leda's ultimate decision isn't one of those vaunted "choices" feminists are always talking about, I don't know what is. Her unequivocal stance contradicts their sacred tenet of Having It All, but life for a woman is such a minefield of conflicts that misanthropy, at least in the figurative sense of "everybody buzz off," is the only thing that really works.

The Prodigal Women contains 556 pages of very small print to accommodate the wartime paper shortage. I first read it from early morning to past midnight for two days in November 1957. I was twenty-one and living alone in an apartment whose rent of seventy-five dollars a month I could barely afford, but that weekend shines in my memory as the happiest interlude of my life.

The weather was blustery and cold, the trees gaunt and bent as the wind stripped off the last of their wet brown leaves. Each time I got up to fix another cup of coffee, I leaned on the kitchen windowsill while I waited for the water to boil, gazing out at the grim day and wrapped in deep pleasure as my mind echoed John Donne's line, "In Heaven, it's always autumn."

OUR LADY'S JUGGLER
SHRUGGED ON THE
INSTALLMENT PLAN

Most misanthropes are easy to understand because we blurt out the simple truths that most people think but never say. The plainspoken have nothing to lose but their friends, so we weigh the risks and behave accordingly.

The exceptional misanthrope, for one reason or another, is driven to spin tangled webs of denial, contradiction, and displacement. Three such puzzles are Anatole France, Ayn Rand, and Louis-Ferdinand Auguste Destouches, who took for his pseudonym his mother's maiden name: Céline.

Anatole France (1844–1924) is the French writer known to everyone who has ever dipped into the ubiquitous paperback, *Great Short Stories of the World*. It always includes "The Procurator of Judea," about two retired Roman bureaucrats talking shop. At the end, one man tries to prompt the other's memory about an incident in Judea during the reign of Tiberius. You were there then, weren't you? You remember that, don't you? But the old procurator shakes his head. "Jesus? Jesus of Nazareth? No, I don't recall," mumbles Pontius Pilate.

When this story was published in 1892, Anatole France was hailed for his pitiless irony and called the "new Voltaire." This in itself was ironic, for irony was no more consistent a trait in him than any of his other traits.

He had my third-year French class in tears when we read a very different short story by him, *"Le Jongleur de Notre Dame,"* about an ignorant, probably retarded, itinerant juggler who passes through a village during its festival in honor of the Virgin Mary.

As the juggler watches in awe, each villager pays homage to the Virgin in his own way and according to his own talents. The village carpenter makes her a new manger, the seamstress makes her a new robe, and so on, placing their tributes before the fine new statue of the Virgin in the village church.

Deeply touched by their devotion, the juggler wants to pay homage to the Virgin too, but how? Juggling is all he knows. Going into the church at night when no one else is there, he performs in front of the statue as he has never performed before. Leaping, spinning, standing on his head, he gives his all in such a tour de force that at last, covered with sweat, he collapses in exhaustion.

Suddenly the door bursts open and the villagers, who have been spying on him, rush in and attack him for committing a sacrilege. But just as they are about to kill him, the statue comes to life and the Virgin Mary steps down from her pedestal and wipes the sweat from the juggler's face with her veil.

The author of this reverent story was the same Anatole France who supported Dreyfus because the Church was anti-Dreyfus and he hated the Church. His books are full of sentiments such as, "Men are the most pernicious race of little odious vermin that

Nature ever suffered to crawl upon the face of the earth," yet his eulogy at Zola's funeral concluded with a line that has been cherished and quoted by humanitarians ever since: "He was a moment of the conscience of mankind."

Misanthropes are born, not made. A traumatic childhood seems to have no more effect on the formation of the misanthropic temperament than a happy childhood, but Anatole France may have been inconsistent in this as well. An early biographer, Barry Cerf, writing five years after his death, paints a classic Oedipal situation in his 1929 study, *Anatole France: The Degeneration of a Great Writer*. I suspect that Cerf was influenced by the Freudian craze sweeping the twenties, but that's all right. No one caught in the storm that was Anatole France can afford to be fussy about ports.

He was born Jacques-Anatole Thibault. His father, a bookseller on the quais of Paris, was a staunch Catholic, militarist, and royalist, the latter possibly explaining why his son took his country's name for a pseudonym. Papa also seems to have had a great deal to do with the atheism, dilettantism, socialism, communism, reactionism, and patriotism that turned up in Anatole at various times, and occasionally all at once.

His mother was a sentimentalist of the same degree as those overheated women who made pilgrimages to Rousseau's tomb to contemplate the wonders of *sensibilité*. Anatole's assessment of her is not for the fainthearted:

She literally poisoned my life. She made me inconsistent and timid. . . . Love brought the most honest woman in the world to commit acts of the most revolting indelicacy. . . . Until I was thirty-five, she never went to bed until I came home. . . . To the time of my marriage my mother tucked me into bed every night. When she had kissed me and was carrying away the candle, I sometimes longed to strangle her. There is no more heavy tyranny than mother-love.

Schopenhauer was also a misanthrope and his mother threw him down a flight of stairs, so what can you do? At least Frau Schopenhauer was of this world, whereas Mme Thibault floated around in one of her own making in which everybody was sweet and nice. Writes Cerf: "France's youthful idealism, founded as it was on an unstable basis, collapsed. . . . Had he not dreamed away his childhood and youth, had he learned earlier that human beings are neither saints nor paladins, he might have been able to reconcile himself to the sad facts of life and the dreary mediocrity of mankind when the truth finally forced itself through his doting mother's guard."

One result of Anatole's years under his doting mother's guard had my fourth-year French class in tears. *Le Livre de Mon Ami* is a collection of vignettes about the happy childhood of what even I called "a darling little boy." It was the only time in my life that I have ever loved children, an inconsistency I owe to Anatole France.

He finally got out from under his mother, or as he put it: "And then I married. After the sacrament I learned what hell is."

Although he was already middle-aged in the 1880s, he was drawn to Oscar Wilde's Aestheticism and Ernest Renan's Dilettantism, both of which provided him with the attitudes he needed to cope with his father-mother split. The watchwords of these literary movements were *light* irony, *tolerant* skepticism, *nonchalant* aloofness—in sum, the Mauve Decade's version of "cool."

He achieved the requisite tone in his first novel, *The Crime of Sylvestre Bonnard,* whose *gently* witty protagonist says things like: "He hated fanaticism, but he was fanatically tolerant." Next came *Thais,* about a fifth-century Christian monk and an Alexandrian courtesan who pull the same kind of switch on each other as the young couple in O. Henry's "Gift of the Magi," except that Anatole adds a cutting edge. The monk keeps trying to convert Thais to Christianity at the same time she keeps trying to convert him to sensuality. It goes on like this until the very end, when the monk finally loses his faith and heads for Thais's bed, only to discover that she has finally seen the light and become a Christian.

Anatole lost his cool a few years later in *The Opinions of Jerome Coignard,* whose protagonist is a dramatized representation of French thought in the Age of Reason. A bleak realist, Coignard charges the leaders of the Revolution with naiveté and counters their optimistic opinions of mankind with his own: "He would not have signed a line of the Declaration of the Rights of Man because of the excessive and iniquitous distinction that is established in it between man and the gorilla."

From now on, Anatole vows to be an Age of Reason man, a skeptic who sees human nature as it is, not as it ought to be. Using Jerome Coignard as a mouthpiece, he condemns Rousseau for promoting the inherent goodness of human nature: "He who undertakes to guide men must never lose sight of the fact that they are malicious monkeys. . . . The folly of the Revolution was in aiming to establish virtue on the earth. When you want to make men good and wise, free, moderate, generous, you are led inevitably to the desire of killing them all." As for making them think, their reaction to intelligence could be observed by "pouring ammonia on an anthill."

Rejecting Rousseau's political ideas, he clung to Rousseau's sexy ideas, such as "confidence in the superiority of instinct, the senses, sentiment, emotion, and the superiority of all these to reason, reflection, and intelligence." This exercise in the impossible made Anatole a romantic realist, a primitive rationalist, and a tender misanthrope of the naked intellect, but he saved his best leap of logic for the Dreyfus case. Insisting that he was still a reactionary, he aligned himself with the Dreyfusards against church, state, and the Army of France.

The revelations of the Dreyfus case increased his misanthropy. "I am persuaded that the sum of stupidity and folly in the world is at all times constant," he wrote. "Far from rejoicing when I see an old error depart, I think of the new error which will come to take its place, and I wonder anxiously if it will not be more inconvenient or more dangerous than the first." On this pessimistic note, he threw in his lot with human progress and became a socialist.

The work he published during his socialist period contains his bitterest condemnations of mankind. *Penguin Island* is an all-out attack on French society; *The Gods Athirst* presents a right-wing view of the Revolution that shocked republicans; and *The Revolt of the Angels,* in which angels and devils change places, expresses a savage and unrelieved loathing for the entire human race.

When France entered World War I on August 1, 1914, the seventy-year-old Anatole, who, being a socialist, was an antimilitarist and a pacifist, presented himself at the army recruitment center and demanded a rifle.

His attempts to explain his contradictions only manufactured more. Drawn to Pascal's distinction between pity that leads to sympathy and pity that leads to contempt, he came up with "tender spite" and "benevolent scorn" to describe his attitudes, using the confusing phrases so often in interviews that the critics eventually picked them up and used them in reviews.

An illogical Frenchman is a frightening spectacle and virtually a contradiction in terms. Logic is sacred in the land of Descartes but Anatole's thought patterns seem custom-tailored for America, land of post hocky ergo propter hocky, where Occam's razor wouldn't cut butter. With his gift for oxymorons, if he were resurrected he could go on Oprah and join the gang discussion of "tough love" without missing a beat.

Anatole won the Nobel Prize for literature in 1921. This honor can ruin a misanthrope because the unspoken ground rule for laureates is: "If you can't say something nice about Man with a capital M, don't say anything at all." The pressure is so grand-motherly that a laureate runs the risk of never being the same sonofabitch again, but Anatole wriggled free. Barely a year after his Stockholm triumph he was saying: "I have rarely opened a door by mistake without discovering a spectacle which made me look upon humanity with pity, disgust, or horror."

Summing him up, Cerf calls him "a sensualist to whom love meant carnal desire," who had "little that was fine or lovable in his character. . . . he was not kindly, generous, or even tol-erant. . . . while he was surrounded by scores of ecstatic ad-mirers and numerous acquaintances, he seems to have had no devoted friends."

Yet his ultimate contradiction, Cerf believes, contains the key to his personality: "Despite his contempt for man and man's affairs, he loved life intensely."

This view would seem to be supported by the words of one of Anatole's fictional characters: "This dog's life. . . . I love it, brutal, vile, and gross; I love it sordid, unclean, decayed; I love it stupid, half-witted and cruel; I love it in its obscenity, in its ignominy, in its infamy, with its impurity, its hideousness, and its squalor, its corruption and its stench."

A neat evasion, and one calculated to charm romanticists with its Rousseauistic touches, but I don't believe it. Anatole's politi-cal and philosophical inconsistencies had their roots in the ulti-mate inconsistency of trying all his life to combine misanthropy and sensuality.

The misanthrope must either be cold to begin with, or he must turn cold when he finally acknowledges what he has known all along: Sex requires people. There is no greater contradiction than a misanthrope in bed. If he persists in staying there, the primal contradiction will spread like a cancer to his higher brain cells, until nothing he says or thinks will make any sense.

Consistency, thou art a jewel. As with Catholicism, so with misanthropy, the jewel in the crown is celibacy.

Another life-loving misanthrope fled Soviet Russia for America in 1926. Twenty-one-year-old Alice Rosenbaum arrived in New York lugging a Remington-Rand typewriter and some books by a Finnish writer whose surname was Ayn.

Years later as Ayn Rand she would define her philosophy of Objectivism as "the concept of man as a heroic being, with his own happiness as the moral purpose of his life, with productive achievement as his noblest activity, and reason as his only absolute." She devised an oath to this effect and put it into the mouth of the hero of *Atlas Shrugged:* "I swear by my life, and by my love of it, that I will never live for the sake of another man, nor ask another man to live for mine."

Her father's drugstore chain had been taken over by the Soviets in the name of the People, so Ayn's mother sold her jewelry to send her daughter to America. Taken in by her Chicago cousins, she immediately took possession of their cramped apartment in the name of Ayn Rand. A night owl like most writers, she kept her cousins awake with her midnight-to-dawn typing and used up all their hot water for her frequent baths—which she also took at night, running the water full blast until the tub was nice and full.

If her cousins were disturbed, it did not matter because she rejected familial ties. People just happen to be born into a particular family, she believed, and this element of chance made of consanguinity an "unchosen value." Loving one's family or behaving differently toward them simply because they were family was therefore "irrational."

It was a consummately un-Jewish attitude, but Rand also rejected Jewishness in the same sweeping way. Although she was born in Czarist Russia in 1905 and raised in St. Petersburg, she told her biographer Barbara Branden that she had never met with the slightest manifestation of anti-Semitism, nor heard any discussion of it at home. This conflicts with another story she told Branden: that her father had become a pharmacist because the only available Jewish quota at the university was in chemistry, and eager for an education, he took it even though his real interests were history and literature.

In *The Passion of Ayn Rand,* Branden posits that since anti-Semitism was ubiquitous in Russia during Rand's childhood, she had to have encountered it, but probably blocked it out of her mind "because the memory would have carried with it an unacceptable feeling of humiliation." She never denied that she was a Jew, but "it had no significance to her, she had no emotional tie or sense of identification with Jews or things Jewish." Like family ties, Jewishness conflicted with Rand's belief that "man is a being of self-made soul," so she chose to be unchosen.

Rand's Chicago uncle, who was in the movie-distributing business, gave her a letter of introduction to Cecil B. DeMille and she headed for Hollywood with her silent-movie screenplays. Working as an extra and a properties reader, she met a young bit player named Frank O'Connor and fell in love with him at first sight. He was the physical type she went for: "American-looking," as she often said: tall, blond, blue-eyed, long-legged, slim.

He was also an American citizen, and Rand's visa was running out. They were married in Los Angeles and went to Mexico on their honeymoon so that she could re-enter the United States as his wife. Later on she would joke, "Ours was a shotgun wedding—with Uncle Sam holding the shotgun." Barbara Branden believes that this was pretty much the case. She says the couple's early Hollywood friends felt that Frank was not particularly in love with Ayn, and that "everybody knew" he married her so she would not be sent back to Soviet Russia—a selfless act of the sort that Rand would one day castigate in her novels as "altruism."

Now that she had her man, she had to make sure he fit the heroic mold that was the basis of her developing philosophy. Recalling the first time she saw him, she told Braden: "he was enormously anti-social—and of course I liked that. His manner suggested an aloof, confident self-sufficiency. I never caught him speaking to anyone, he always sat alone. . . ."

Rand's capacity for believing what she wished to believe was boundless. As Branden and everyone else who knew Frank quickly discovered, he was actually passive; a sweet, gentle, thoughtful man who was overwhelmed by his dogmatic, self-absorbed wife. He stopped working as soon as Rand began making enough to support them, and gradually became the "wife" while she became the "husband." However much this role reversal conflicted with Rand's heroic philosophy, it suited her on a personal level because she hated women.

"In childhood, all of her life, it appears that her most intense scorn was reserved for women," Branden writes. "The human qualities she cared about were, she believed, specifically masculine attributes: above all, purposefulness and strength."

Rand's hatred of the female role turns up in cloaked form in all her novels. The oath from *Atlas Shrugged* would make an apt masthead motto for *MS*. Howard Roark's final speech in *The Fountainhead* opens with, "I am a man who does not exist for others." Her most detestable villain, Ellsworth Toohey, preaches "the nobility of self-sacrifice in order to rob men of their self-esteem, their courage, their virtue, and their honor and to turn them into willing sacrificial victims"—a passage that needs only one word changed to fit any feminist tract, or to state the theme of *The Cinderella Complex.* Communism itself, with its demands for selfless dedication, undoubtedly reminded her of the demands made upon her sex, and the many women, contemptible to her, who met them.

After the publication of *The Fountainhead* brought her to the attention of conservative intellectuals, a friend told her that the Austrian economist Ludwig von Mises had called her "the most courageous man in America." "Did he say *man?*" asked Rand. Assured that von Mises had indeed said *man,* she was overjoyed.

In everyday life she was a fearful woman who poured boiling water on the dishes to kill germs, worried whether she had locked the door, hated to fly, and could not learn to drive. Obsessed with the need to have full control of her destiny, she was afraid, says Branden, "that she might inadvertently fail to take precautions against an external danger that could be averted."

Called "Mrs. Logic" by Nathaniel Branden, Rand boasted that her philosophy of Objectivism was so tightly reasoned that a person who accepted even the smallest part of it had to accept all of it. Those who did not she called "hooligans"—a favorite epithet of Communism that she evidently picked up in spite of herself—and accused them of "vicious dishonesty," "moral treason," and "social metaphysics" (going along with the crowd instead of being an individualist).

With the connivance of Nathaniel Branden, head of the New York-based Objectivist Institute and chief gremlin of the happy few allowed to sit at her feet, social metaphysicians were actually put on trial in Rand's living room and sent away to reflect on their "volitionally chosen cancer of the spirit"—her redundant name for any opinion she disagreed with.

Rand cloaked her misanthropy in various lesser guises: aloofness and intimidating formality, the half-loaf of misogyny, and contempt, "a term she used again and again to describe her feelings for most of the people around her," writes Barbara Branden. "It is a term that—accompanied by a dismissive wave of her hand and a grimace of distaste—dotted her conversations." She advised her followers, "Don't withhold your contempt from men's vices," a practice she herself followed so often that she was constantly breaking off relations with friends of many years' standing. Said one: "She seemed almost to invite a break, as though it would confirm her attitude toward the world."

These ruptures were invariably cerebral rather than emotional. Ostracism awaited those who expressed admiration for a writer, painter, or composer that Rand considered "irrational." She decreed that Van Gogh was "wild," Rembrandt was full of "grim, unfocused malevolence," Beethoven had a "tragic sense of doom," Shakespeare was an "abysmal failure" because his characters were swept along by their emotions instead of being ruled by reason and free will, and Somerset Maugham's *Of Human Bondage* expressed "a deeply malevolent view of life."

She hated nature lovers so much that she almost threw Barbara Branden out of the house for saying that she enjoyed scenery. To Rand, nature was not only wild and irrational, just as Rousseau said, but also "malevolent," another of her favorite words for anything that did not lend itself to intellectual order and control.

She carried misanthropy of the naked intellect further than it has ever been carried before or since. Anyone who *dared* say a good word for nature had to listen to Rand sing the praises of skyscrapers, concrete, steel girders, smokestacks, and even industrial smoke, for these were the products of the rational mind of Man, who invented them. The individual unwise enough to suggest that these things are inanimate had to sit up until 4 A.M. listening to Rand explain why a blast furnace symbolized an "exalted sense of life."

Everything good was a product of rationalism; all evil proceeded from irrationalism, including cancer: its cause, she believed, was "bad premises."

Blaise Pascal called Man "a thinking reed," but Ayn Rand had no use for reediness. Her fictional heroes are perfect; morally incorruptible, dedicated geniuses with stratospheric levels of exaltation and such stringent ideals that they are as chaste as Hippolytus until the right woman comes along. Reviled and punished by an envious world, they are so secure in their egoism that they never for a moment consider misanthropy as a response to their very real troubles. In *The Fountainhead,* the man who has ruined Howard Roark's reputation and career asks him, "What do you think of me, Mr. Roark?" "I don't think of you," Roark replies.

Randian heroes are ideal candidates for misanthropy of the naked intellect but they never get elected. No matter what they suffer at the hands of people, Rand cannot permit them to hate people because she has drawn them above the battle. The closest she comes to creating an overtly misanthropic character is *The Fountainhead*'s Dominique Francon, of whom she said, "Dominique is myself in a bad mood." The real misanthropes in Rand's novels are the professional people lovers: altruists, humanitarians, social workers, labor leaders, public relations flacks, one worlders, collectivists, socialists, and conformists—in short, tender misanthropes with bad premises.

Mrs. Logic painted herself into a corner. She couldn't admit that she hated people because that would class her with her fictional bad guys, yet if she identified with her good guys—which of course she did—she still couldn't admit that she hated people because her good guys love Man.

She was also stymied by her inordinate self-love, which made the misanthrope's unavoidable philosophical trap repugnant to her. If the human race is no damn good, the misanthrope, being a member of it, is no damn good either. The way out of this is to have a taste for irony and an appreciation of the ridiculous, but she had neither. Barbara Branden recalls "the chastening experience of telling her a joke . . . then being greeted by a blank look of bewilderment—then having to give a lengthy explanation of what was the presumed humor." Rand was suspicious of humor on principle, says Branden, especially the idea of being able to laugh at oneself, a suggestion that drew from her the stony reply: "That's the man who wants a blank check on flaws."

Unable to admit her misanthropy without destroying her Man-centered philosophy, Rand clung to her philosophy and got meaner and meaner from the frustration growing out of her conflict. "Her vision of the human potential made the rest of reality unendurable," writes Branden. Creating paragons on paper made her expect the impossible from the actual people around her. At the age of sixty-three she expected thirty-seven-year-old Nathaniel Branden to find her sexually desirable because she was his "highest value." When her husband turned into a drunk from living with her, she claimed that "his problems were psycho-epistemological" and made him write papers on his thought processes, refusing to believe that there could be anything wrong with his sense of exalted purpose.

Atlas Shrugged finally forced Ayn Rand to confront her misanthropy. In *We the Living,* her autobiographical first novel set in early Soviet Russia, the villains are Communists, a large group as political movements go but by no means a majority of mankind. In her second novel, *The Fountainhead,* the villains are conformists, a larger group but still manageable, especially in post-World War II America, when many other thinkers were bewailing conformity. But in *Atlas Shrugged* the villains are mediocre people, the world's largest majority. Like the aristocrat who hates the masses, she made it in on numbers.

"Makes well-poisoning seem like one of the kindlier arts," wrote reviewer Gore Vidal.

". . . an outpouring of hate," charged Patricia Donegan in *The Commonweal.*

Granville Hicks in the *New York Times:* "Loudly as Miss Rand proclaims her love of life, it seems clear that the book is written out of hate. . . ."

Barbara Branden finds in *Atlas* "a blistering contempt for the world," and speculates: "On a more subtle level, her hatred seemed to be rooted in a deep, terrible fear—as if the outside world was not merely an arena where wrong ideas were held and wrong actions taken: it was an arena fraught with danger."

What was it? Studying this passage, I detect something that Barbara Branden missed in this otherwise superb biography: Ayn Rand's whole shtik was a gargantuan displacement of her never-admitted fear of anti-Semitism.

Her hatred of the irrational, her construction of a laborious philosophy based on individualism, reason, logic, objective thinking, and rejection of emotionalism would, if universally adopted, bring about an immediate end to anti-Semitism, which is a product of the Gentile id. By constructing fictional plots in which logical behavior and rational characters always triumph over the forces of darkness, she spent her entire career as a novelist crusading against anti-Semitism while taking care not to write a word about Jews.

There is not a single Jewish character in all of her work; not even in *We the Living,* which is set in Russia, or in *The Fountainhead,* which is set entirely in Manhattan. She admitted that she modeled architecture critic and free-lance humanitarian Ellsworth Toohey chiefly on Harold Laski, yet Toohey is a Wasp. With the exception of the heroes, to whom she gave Irish names (Roark, Rearden, Galt) in honor of Frank O'Connor, everybody, good or bad, is a Wasp. Peter Keating and Jim Taggart are rats but they are Wasp rats; Gail Wynand was raised in a Hell's Kitchen tenement but he's Wasp; and Dominique Francon, despite her frenchified name, is the procelain Wasp debutante incarnate.

Moreover, they all look Wasp. Toohey is the drip with the bookbag, but everyone else is long and lanky, blond or carrottop, blue- or gray-eyed. The partial exception is the handsome villain Peter Keating, who has black hair and gains weight. By the time she wrote *Atlas Shrugged* Rand seemed to have recognized the need for a little ethnic variety, but what did she name the heroic pirate who hijacks ships carrying humanitarian aid? Ragnar Danneskjold—just what the copy editor needed.

Despite their overwhelming Gentileness, Randian heroes come off as metaphors for Jews because they are beset by irrational forces that try to bar them from the professions and use their virtues against them to bring about their destruction—what Rand, in a rare unguarded moment, called "the sanction of the victim," a phrase that reminds us of the language of the Holocaust debate.

The major heroes are never permitted to exhibit or even acknowledge the existence of anything that could be construed as Jewish agony. Instead, they analyze their problems coldly and declaim them in long speeches like characters in the neoclassical dramas of Corneille and Racine. But a minor hero of *The Foun-*

tainhead gives it away. New York Wasp sculptor Stephen Mallory's definition of terror echoes the age-old keening *why?* of the persecuted Jew that pervades Bernard Malamud's *The Fixer,* whose real-life model was in a Czarist prison when Ayn Rand was a child in Russia:

> To me—it's being left, unarmed, in a sealed cell with a drooling beast of prey or a maniac who's had some disease that's eaten his brain out. You'd have nothing then but your voice—your voice and your thought. You'd scream to that creature why it should not touch you, you'd have the most eloquent words, the unanswerable words, you'd become the vessel of the absolute truth. And you'd see the living eyes watching you and you'd know that the thing can't hear you, that it can't be reached, not reached, not in any way, yet it's breathing and moving there before you with a purpose of its own.

Barbara Branden writes that Rand regarded "the outside world" as a place of peril and wanted "to create a safe haven around her, a smaller world within the larger irrational world that would consist of people who were predictable, intelligible, in accord with her thinking, devoted to her. . . ."

She did in *Atlas Shrugged.* The Wyoming mountain sanctuary, Atlantis or "Galt's Gulch," into which the rational creators and captains of industry disappear and start their own community, is Ayn Rand's Israel. The Anglo-Celtic inhabitants are the Chosen—by Ayn Rand—People, exiles who actually do what the Jews have always been accused of doing: running the world.

Louis Ferdinand Auguste Destouches (1894–1961), known to the world as Céline, was born and raised behind his mother's lace shop in a canopied arcade near the Paris Opera, which explains much of what you are about to read: the kid lived in a mall.

The flat was grim and dark—literally from the sunless arcade, figuratively from the parsimonious, repressed petit bourgeois mindset that prevailed within. It is easy to imagine the shabby furniture swathed in doilies made from leftover lace. Worse, the family had to eat bland foods like noodles, rice, and bread soup to guard the lace against rich kitchen smells. Céline described all this in his second novel, *Mort à crédit,* translated into English as *Death on the Installment Plan.*

Céline was wounded at Ypres in 1914 and decorated for valor. After the war he resumed his studies at the Rennes Medical School and in 1919 married the dean's daughter. Any other man would have used his father-in-law's connections to feather his nest, but Céline had an aversion to accepting help from anyone. It almost seemed that he had married into an influential medical family solely for the pleasure of spurning their influence; after a few years he took a traveling job as a League of Nations physician and never lived with his wife or their daughter again.

He worked in Geneva, Germany, Cuba, and Detroit, where he studied the medical and psychological aspects of the Ford assembly line. After his American sojourn he returned to Paris, got a job in a free clinic in a workingclass neighborhood, and wrote a novel on the side.

It is here that his resemblance to Somerset Maugham abruptly ends. Maugham emerged from his slum doctoring with a cynical fondness for humanity, but Céline seems to have found in it a justification for his burgeoning misanthropy.

His first novel, *Voyage au bout de la nuit,* rendered in English as *Voyage to the Middle of the Night,* was published in 1932. It's something of an existentialist *Anthony Adverse,* a story of travel and adventure in exotic places by a slum doctor named Bardamu and his friend and alter ego, Robinson, a classic sonofabitch and Social Darwinist who represents the misanthropy that Bardamu feels but can't quite bring himself to express.

The funniest line comes when Robinson tells Bardamu that he understands perfectly why his friend became a doctor: "When people can stand up, they're thinking of killing you. Whereas when they're ill, there's no doubt about it, they're less dangerous." In Part One of the novel, the tormented, confused Bardamu is committed to an insane asylum; when we meet him again in Part Two, he has risen to chief of staff. In the end he admits that the world is mad, but unable to kill himself, he lives on as head of his own private madhouse.

In *Voyage* Céline launched a fusillade against the bourgeoisie, calling it the class that guillotined Louis XVI and then proceeded to treat the common man worse than kings ever had. This made him the darling of the French Left, but as soon as the intellectuals began praising him, he adopted a philistine stance and confided to interviewers: "the very word 'writing' has always struck me as indecent."

Voyage was published in the Soviet Union and Céline was invited, along with Gide and other Communist pets, to visit the Workers' Paradise. The only way he could get his Soviet royalties was to go to Russia and spend the money there, so he went. The Soviets planned to use the visiting French writers for propaganda purposes, but when they asked Céline what he thought of their noble experiment, he told them they were arrogant for thinking they could perfect anything as rotten as mankind.

The only good thing about Christianity, he went on, is that it *tells* man he is inherently evil, so at least the church is honest—unlike Communism, which has the temerity to think that man can be changed. "You have the nerve to dress up a turd and call it a caramel," he said, and then wrapped up the interview with a call for a Franco-German alliance to save France from the Marxist blight.

Returning home, he enlarged upon his Russian comments in a polemic called *Mea culpa*. Published in 1936, it raised a firestorm, not only among the French Left but in polite society generally, because of his remarks about Jews. The bourgeoisie "smells a little Jewish," he wrote, accusing the middle class of cosying up to Léon Blum's Popular Front government for "life insurance." But it really didn't matter, he concluded, because society was so corrupt that "with Jews or without Jews" it was doomed.

Now he became the darling of the French Right, but when he was invited to attend a fascist meeting and the speaker began denouncing the "Jewish-Marxist tyranny," Céline stood up and yelled, "To hell with that Aryan *merde!*" and called the Germans krauts and blockheads. Despite this, Lucien Rebatet, editor of the French fascist newspaper *Je Suis Partout,* asked Céline to write some articles for him. Céline did, but his vituperative racism was too much even for Rebatet and he refused to print them.

No one could figure out where he was coming from. "I adhere only to myself, as much as I can," was the only explanation Céline offered.

He went on to write three more polemics that, as he was later to say, accomplished the impossible: "Left and Right, Monarchist and Communist, all agreed that I was the greatest scum on earth." The polemics, known by the confusing name, "pamphlets," were actually full-length books. They have never been published in English and probably never will be, because they were so full of hate, for Jews and just about everybody else, that they were banned in Nazi Germany.

Bagatelles pour un massacre (trifles for a massacre) rehashed the discredited "Protocols of the Elders of Zion" and claimed

that there was indeed a Jewish conspiracy, not of international bankers as the Protocols claimed, but of two modern centers of Jewish influence: "Hollywood la juive" and "Moscou la youtre."

In *Ecole des cadavres* the corpses are the Gentiles who were slaughtered in World War I and who are destined to be slaughtered again in another war engineered by Jews with the connivance of their special Gentile pets, the English (Céline believed the two had "good chemistry"). He also blamed the coming war on liberals, socialists, idealists, the Frenchman-in-the-street, Masons, the Catholic church, and the Communists. Yet the book was dedicated to a Communist sympathizer, Eugene Dabit, whom Céline happened to like.

The last polemic, published in 1941 after the fall of France, was *Les beaux draps* (a fine mess). Between American Jewish movies and Russian Jewish socialism, Céline wrote, the masses were so brain-dead that they might just as well be exploited because it was all they were good for.

Never one to insult just one side when two were available, he also accused the Vichy government of cowardly opportunism: "I didn't wait for the German High Command to be set up at the Hotel Crillon before becoming pro-German."

After *Bagatelles* Céline was forced out of his job at the government clinic. He lived on his seventy-percent disability pension from his World War I wounds, in a Montmartre apartment overtop the one used by the Resistance. They did not make the connection between Dr. Destouches and the writer named Céline, but Céline knew who they were. His own fascist visitors routinely passed Resistance fighters on the stairs but Céline never reported his downstairs neighbors to the German Occupation; moreover, he treated, free of charge, a Resistance member who fell ill.

As the Allied liberation forces closed in on Paris in 1944 Cé-

line, fearing summary execution, fled to Sigmaringen in the Black Forest where he served as house physician to the Vichy exiles holed up in an ancient Hohenzollern castle. True to form, he refused to make radio broadcasts for the Nazis.

When Paris was liberated he took off again, this time for Denmark where he claimed he had buried some gold in the garden of a former girlfriend. Accompanied by his second wife Lucette, he made his way, sometimes by train, sometimes on foot, across war-torn Germany with his cat Bébert in a woolen bag around his neck.

He never found the gold. After the war ended the French government demanded his extradition. Céline and Lucette were both arrested and jailed in Denmark, she for two months and he for fourteen, while bureaucrats in both countries wrangled over his status. In the end the Danish government refused to extradite him. When he got sick they sent him to a prison hospital for several months, then set him free on condition that he not try to leave Denmark without permission. His Danish lawyer lent Céline and Lucette a cottage on the Baltic where they lived from 1947 until France granted him amnesty in 1951.

He was tried in absentia for collaboration in 1950. It was widely believed by the French public that the "monster of Montmartre" had promoted the Holocaust in his pamphlets, but an American biographer, David O'Connell, who read all four in the original French, states that "nowhere in the text of these works are any such calls for mass murder made."

Morally speaking, this is a minor point. Anyone with Céline's unvarnished opinion of human nature knows that the mass of people can be swung like a lariat and are incapable of making fine distinctions between the theory of anti-Semitism and its ultimate practice: to write the former is to invite the latter. Technically speaking, however, Céline called for the expulsion of Jews

to England, the United States, the Soviet Union, and Palestine.

He was found guilty by a majority of the jurors but the punishment meted out to him was meaningless. He was sentenced to a year in prison, which he had already served; fined 50,000 francs, which he did not have; consigned to "perpetual disgrace," which he was already in; and subjected to the confiscation of his worldly goods, of which he had exactly none.

He returned to France in 1951 and received permission to practice medicine in Menton. At first the literary world maintained a careful silence; later on, when he resumed writing and it became fashionable to say "Céline is a terrible person but a gifted writer," a few supporters like Roger Nimier beat the drums for a Nobel Prize. In 1957 he published *D'un chateau à l'autre* (from one castle to another), a novel about his wartime flight. Various others followed, one dedicated to "Animals, Sick People and Prisoners," and another to Pliny the Elder, who died in the eruption of Vesuvius.

Eerily, he finished his last book a few hours before he died of a sudden massive stroke. Called *Rigadon,* it is an attack on the Chinese. They were going to take over the West, he predicted; Europe was finished and the barbarians were at the gates. He was sure of this, he said, because: "I am a parasitolgist, doctorated!"

Analyzing Céline has become a popular sport. Sartre wrote *Anti-Semite and Jew* with him in mind, but the best comment on his complex personality comes from the lawyer who defended him at his trial: "He was too much of a loner to collaborate with anybody."

Some students of Céline have tried to absolve him of anti-Semitism by claiming that he used Jews merely as a *symbol* of evil, as if that in itself were not anti-Semitic. Some have said that his hatred of Jews was a temporary aberration caused by some personal crisis that just happened to correspond with World War

II; others that he was temporarily insane at this same convenient time. Those of the Freudian persuasion say that he substituted Jews for the parents he hated; other Freudians believe that the image of Jews as beset outsiders was Céline's own image of himself, and he felt they had stolen his show.

Sartre missed by a mile with his venality theory: "If Céline could support the social theses of the Nazis, it is because he was paid to do so." David O'Connell points out that the Soviets tried and failed to get Céline this way, and quotes a witness who was with him in Moscow: "I was highly amused, knowing that Céline, a delicate and honest man, without needs, without vices, without a car, without a servant, a nonsmoker who drank only water, was one of those very rare beings who couldn't be bought."

O'Connell traces Céline's anti-Semitism in part to his origins in the strongly anti-Dreyfus lower middle class, his resentment of Jewish success in medicine, and his unrequited love for an American woman who married a Jew, but he reminds us that all of Céline's behavior owed much to the fact that he was "an eccentric, albeit a vengeful and racist one," whose every act and thought were a "manifestation of his unusually strong spirit of independence."

Here we have a paradox. Anti-Semitism being history's oldest form of groupthink, rugged individualists and eccentrics tend to be its least likely practitioners. Anyone who hears a different drummer probably will be so repelled by the conformity of anti-Semitism and the company that anti-Semites must keep that he might just become a philo-Semite out of contempt for the mass mind.

Why didn't Céline, the consummate eccentric, take this route? Here I must hazard a guess, because of all the misanthropes I examine in this book, Céline is the one who leaves me stumped.

The only thing about him that I can identify with is the fascist-good-neighbor number he did on the Resistance. Basing my theory on what I would do in the same situation, I suspect that he somehow discovered the location of the Resistance apartment and rented another one in the same building purely out of puckishness, delighting in the spectacle of Resistance members and collaborators passing each other on the stairs and exchanging polite greetings—especially the French equivalent of "Have a nice day."

As for his anti-Semitism, I think it was somehow tied up with his laziness.

That he was lazy is indicated by his so-called medical career. He liked to say that he chose to work in government clinics because he could not bear to grow rich from anything as repulsive as sick people, but if he found sick people repulsive, why did he become a doctor at all?

O'Connell believes Céline's clinic work proves that "despite all the shortcomings he found in mankind, he was still committed to helping people without getting rich in the process." That's a generous interpretation but I can't accept it. My guess is that Céline took salaried jobs and appointments to government clinics because it was easier than opening a private practice.

The same penchant for taking the easy way out shows up in his writing. His first novel, *Voyage au bout de la nuit,* is written in a traditional style, but his subsequent works are marred by what he called his "digest" or "telegraphic" method—fragmentary sentences separated by three dots. He claimed that he was trying to capture the way people really think and talk, but as Samuel Johnson pointed out, what is written with ease is never read with pleasure. Céline succeeded in making things easy only for himself.

In the same way, anti-Semitism was easier than misanthropy.

I see the lazy Céline trying to simplify his many hatreds and turn them into a manageable political and intellectual shorthand by using anti-Semitism as a kind of computer mouse.

Armed with his quick 'n' easy mechanical ethic, he moved all over the screen of human nature, finding materialism, arrogance, hypocrisy, manipulation, and exploitation in Communists, socialists, liberals, monarchists, Masons, the church, the middle class, the lower-middle class, the workingclass, the Frenchman-in-the-street, the English, the Germans, the Resistance, the Vichyites, and finally the Chinese—and then dumped it all in the Jew file.

BY FLYING SPIKES IN
F-SHARP POSSESSED

I wish I could say I never met a misanthrope who bored me, but I can't. Three who leave me cold are Ty Cobb, Irving Berlin, and James Gould Cozzens.

Tyrus Raymond Cobb (1886–1961) was born in Royston, Georgia, and named by his scholarly father after the ancient city of Tyre, renowned for having stood up to Alexander the Great.

The Cobbs were big fish in a little pond. W.H. Cobb was a superintendent of schools, newspaper editor, and state senator. His family was a minor branch on the great tree known as the Cobbs of Georgia, who produced the commander of Cobb's Legion (Ashley Wilkes's regiment) in the Civil War. Ty's mother, *née* Chitwood, was the daughter of a well-off landowner. Married to W.H. Cobb when she was only sixteen, she gave him three children, two boys and a girl, of whom Ty was the oldest.

The family was prosperous and Ty's childhood was a Booth Tarkington idyll, although even as a boy he played rough. His father wanted him to become a doctor and Ty rather liked the idea too, but baseball won out. W. H. Cobb, though somewhat disappointed, raised no strenuous objections.

Everything was fine until the night of August 8, 1905, when Mrs. Cobb emptied a .12-gauge double-barreled shotgun into Mr. Cobb, turning him into a pile of shredded meat on the porch.

Eighteen-year-old Ty was in Augusta playing minor-league ball. The two younger children were spending the night with friends, and Mr. Cobb, according to his wife, had left some hours earlier in the family buggy to spend a couple of days supervising some work on his farm. Later that night, however, several people saw him walking around in town.

Mrs. Cobb said she had gone to bed in the room she shared with her husband when she was awakened by a noise and saw the shadow of a man through the tall French windows that led onto the upstairs porch. Although it was a hot Georgia night, the windows were closed and locked. Thinking that the shadowy male figure was a stranger trying to break in, she grabbed the loaded shotgun that was kept by the bed and fired once. Neighbors testified that they heard the blast, and then, "a considerable time later," heard another.

Mrs. Cobb said she went to the shattered window and saw her husband lying in a pool of blood. The family doctor, who was the first to see the body, found a loaded revolver in the dead man's pocket.

Ty was summoned from Augusta and came home to tragedy and triumph: no sooner had he arrived back in Royston than a telegram arrived saying that he had been picked up by the Detroit Tigers and had to report at the end of August.

He did, playing his first major-league season while his mother, out on bail, awaited trial for manslaughter. He returned for the trial—she was acquitted—and soon thereafter made a home for her and his sister in Detroit, where they lived for many years. Although he must have heard the Royston gossip about his mother's alleged lover, he never spoke of it to anyone and remained a dutiful son.

In the following season of 1906, a never-identified illness took Ty out of the Tigers line-up for a time. Rumors went round that he was in a mental institution, but he was seen sitting in the stands watching games on numerous occasions. This mystery, like the circumstances of his father's death, has never been entirely cleared up.

After the 1906 season, Ty began what was to be the longest mean streak in baseball. Assessments of his disposition ranged from Tristram Coffin's rather elegant "a creature without normal motivation" to the more usual jock inarticulateness of Jimmy Austin, who said Ty was "real nasty" on the field.

Ty himself explained his behavior in typical Southern fashion: "I was just a mild-mannered Sunday School boy, but those old-timers turned me into a snarling wildcat." There is a good deal of truth to this. All rookies are teased and made the butt of practical jokes, but Ty's Southernness drew more than the usual amount of fire. The Civil War was only forty years in the past when he entered major-league baseball, and the great majority of players were Irish- or German-Catholic boys from the North. The Wasp Ty with his thick Georgia drawl was a natural target; his teammates ganged up on him, sawing his bats in half, cutting up his uniforms, and hitting him with wet newspapers.

He did not take teasing well, and this too is understandable to anyone who knows Southern men. The touchy pride, the almost universal self-image of the beau sabreur, and the underlying conviction that aristocrats pop off quicker than ordinary people, had to be major ingredients in Ty's psyche.

Put off by his smoldering, chip-on-the-shoulder moods, his

teammates gave him the cold treatment, refusing to sit next to him in the dugout and ignoring him on road trips. He ate alone in strange cities and took solitary after-dinner walks, armed with the pistol he always carried and even slept with, thinking about baseball and how to improve his game. The only breaks in his isolation were bare-chested fist fights with other players whom he invited to his hotel room for that purpose. One opponent was Buck Herzog, whose head Ty banged against the floor until some Tigers pulled them apart. Afterwards, a chastened Herzog told the St. Louis Browns: "Ty likes a funny story. I want you guys to think of some good yarns to tell him before the game. Keep him in a good humor."

Ty's philosophy was simple: "Baseball is a red-blooded sport for red-blooded men. It's no pink tea, and mollycoddles had better stay out. It's a struggle for supremacy, a survival of the fittest."

His object was "a general demoralization of the opposing team." This he achieved by spiking infielders as he slid into a base and sending them limping off the field with their stockings hanging in bloody shreds. But he had other, more subtle methods, such as head games that he played with the icy expertise of a KGB psychiatrist. Picking out an emotionally vulnerable player on an opposing team, Ty would pretend to make friends with him; then, when the player felt confident enough to step into the Tigers dugout before the game to say hello, Ty would turn on him in fury, screaming, "Get away from me! Don't talk to me or I'll kill you!" The hapless victim was so shaken that he could not keep his mind on the game or his eye on the ball.

Ty had nothing but contempt for kind-hearted Walter Johnson, the Washington Senators pitcher who refused to brush back batters for fear of killing them with his lethal fastball. Other pitchers, victims of the war of nerves Ty brought to base stealing, were not so kind. A group of them entered into a conspiracy to finish him off with a "beanball" but they soon regretted their decision. Whenever a pitcher threw too far inside, the Georgia Peach would lay a bunt down the first-base line to make him field it, and then collide with him as hard as he could in hopes of breaking his pitching arm. "The baserunner has the right of way," Ty explained, "and the man who blocks it does so at his peril."

He was "the dirtiest player in baseball," said Connie Mack of the Philadelphia Athletics, and the City of Brotherly Love responded accordingly. Heckling Ty was a Shibe Park speciality, but one day a fan went too far and called him a "half-nigger." Ty exploded, leaped into the stands, ran twelve rows up to where the vocal fan sat, and pulled the man out of his seat. He was a printer who had lost all of one hand and some fingers from the other in a shop accident. As Ty began beating him, someone yelled, "He doesn't have any hands!" Ty yelled back, "I don't care if he doesn't have any feet!" and went on with the thrashing.

He was suspended for the rest of the season, causing the first players strike in major-league history. The Tigers hired semi-pro players as scabs, but when they lost to the Athletics 24-2, Ty told his teammates to play, saying he did not want to hurt their careers. It was probably the only time in his life that he functioned as a peacemaker; the Tigers management showed their appreciation by getting his suspension reduced to ten days and fining him fifty dollars.

Ty's most recent biographer, Charles C. Alexander, writes: "Behaving as most of us would like to were we not bound by convention and our own timidity, Cobb both fascinated people and made them uneasy." It's hard not to admire Ty's scrappiness on the diamond where his adversaries were his equals, but admiration recedes under the vast catalogue of his off-field fights, which were almost always with the little people.

In Detroit he beat up the black groundskeeper, who he said was drunk; when the man's wife came running to his rescue, Ty grabbed her by the throat and started choking her. He might have killed her had not the Tigers catcher intervened and pulled them apart.

On another occasion he stepped into some wet concrete and took umbrage at the black laborer who yelled a warning at him. Ty knocked the man down and was charged with assault and battery. He was found guilty and given a suspended sentence, and later gave the laborer seventy-five dollars to avoid a civil suit.

In Cleveland he got into a knife fight with a hotel elevator operator and a night watchman, playing a doubleheader the next day with his face swathed in bandages. When the hotel employees swore out a warrant against him for "cutting with intent to kill," the Tigers front office paid the men's medical bills and offered them hush money, which so enraged a Cleveland detective that he vowed to yank Ty off any train the moment it crossed into Ohio. The Peach spent the rest of the season sitting out Indians games and bypassing the Buckeye State by taking trains into Canada to get back and forth from Detroit to major-league cities on the east coast.

Philadelphians made dozens of death threats against him. Each time the Tigers played the A's, Shibe Park stationed cops in the visitors' dugout and in the right-field bleachers to protect Ty when he played his position. One time a crowd gathered in front of his hotel but he walked defiantly into it until, seeing the famous glint in his eye, the would-be lynch mob parted and let him pass.

In Detroit as he was driving to the railroad station, three men jumped on the running board of his car and hit at him through the window. Leaping out, Ty took them all on, pistol-whipped one of them unconscious, and got stabbed in the back. With blood soaking through his jacket, he made the train just in time and got three hits in the game the next day.

Learning that the grocer refused to give his wife a refund for some spoiled fish, he grabbed his gun and ran to the store. The grocer relented and apologized but it wasn't over yet. Hearing the loud argument, a store employee emerged from a back room to see what was going on. The employee happened to be black, and because he was a butcher, he happened to have a meat cleaver in his hand. It was all Ty needed; he pistol-whipped the butcher and spent the night in jail. Plea: guilty. Fine: fifty dollars.

In Atlanta he got into an argument with a waitress over his check and the cashier hit him over the head with a glass dish. When the cops came, Ty wrestled them to the ground and demanded that they take him to the station in a taxi instead of the police wagon. They agreed.

His wife left him, thereby earning a place on his "Sonofabitch List" that he always carried with him. Some of the others on it were baseball commissioner Kenesaw Mountain Landis, Dutch Leonard, and as time went on, Eleanor Roosevelt and the entire Democratic party.

Advancing age did not stale his infinite monotony. He even started a fight at the Cooperstown Hall of Fame when he thought somebody had snubbed him. Brooding on the incident, he got drunk and spilled a platter of roast beef into the lap of a dinner companion.

Not surprisingly, he was a gun nut with a passion for blood sports. Writing in 1956 when Ty was still alive, biographer John McCallum describes the Peach holding court at his Nevada hunting lodge:

Ty would sit in a big easy chair, smoke rings curling around his lean head and bronzed features, and dream of the big game he was going to hunt some day in Africa. He was going to do that for years, but he never got closer to the jungles with a gun than Canada. But he dreamed on. Plans were changed and rechanged. Bears, mountain lions, and moose fell before his crack shooting on preparatory trips. He wanted those elephants, crocodiles and rhinos, but something else always came up to postpone the expedition. Still he didn't do too badly. His Lake Tahoe lodge is covered with animals he has killed, bear skins, tanned deer hides, and mounted wild mountain goat heads. He prided himself on being able to take young fellows out and "walk 'em down." He went after birds on horseback, hunted fox at night, and dropped deer with his rifle from a moving speed boat.

The year before he died, Ty summoned a ghost writer to Lake Tahoe with the intention of dictating his memoirs, but nothing came of it. Instead he turned the writer into a combination nursemaid and hostage, nearly frightening him to death by firing a pistol into a motel parking lot, and dragging him on a gambling foray to Reno, where Ty spent his time fighting with waitresses, cashiers, bartenders, maids, and any other breed of little people he could find.

I know this man. I saw him many times during my roadhouse-crawling days in Mississippi and North Carolina, and he always looked the same: a round-faced, pink-cheeked gnome of a man, a mean good ole boy biding his time until somebody had the misfortune to make eye contact with him. That's *all* it takes.

The Southerner's famous mean streak is usually attributed to a murky sadomasochism involving fears and fantasies of interracial sex, but I suspect it is really a reaction against the demands of Southern hospitality.

South Carolina novelist Blanche McCrary Boyd writes: "Southerners are as polite as cattle, except when they're not. When they're not, they might shoot you or chase you around the yard with a hatchet." Living up to a reputation is an exhausting business. It is humanly impossible to be as gracious as Southerners are supposed to be, but we long ago got in too deep. The rest of the country came to believe our propaganda and, fatally, we came to believe it ourselves.

In consequence, we produced monsters of hospitality who cast a pall of incessant, unbearable niceness over the entire region. All classes participated in the torture. The aristocratic prototype of hospitality is the crystalline great lady of whom it is said, "She's kindness itself." The plain-folks prototype was my grandmother, the *miles gloriosus* of the spare cot, constantly braying "We'll *make* room!" and issuing jocular threats about what she would do to a guest who even thought about leaving too soon ("I'll just tie you right up and keep you here!").

Hospitality carried to such extremes is bound to create its opposite, and so we produced the misanthropic good ole boy who greeted out-of-state travelers with speeding tickets or unmarked graves, depending upon his mood. If Ty Cobb had not been a ballplayer he would have made a great Georgia sheriff.

The man who put a song in our hearts and a lilt in our steps was a cold-blooded, foul-tempered, tight-fisted monster. The kindest assessment of him comes from Sid Caesar, who said, "Irving Berlin has an instinct for self-preservation." More typical is composer Harry Warren's quip at the end of World War II: "They bombed the wrong Berlin."

Moses and Lena Baline and their six children left Russia for America in 1893 when Israel, the youngest, was five. Later, when Izzy Baline had become Irving Berlin, he liked to say, "Everyone should have a Lower East Side in their lives." The remark illustrates his blindsided egoism. Young enough to adapt to a new country, he flourished in an environment that turned his parents and siblings into *farloyrene menshen,* "lost souls who spent the balance of their days in a trance of alienation and drudgery," says biographer Laurence Bergreen in *As Thousands Cheer.*

At thirteen Izzy quit school and left home to sing in saloons and live in Bowery flophouses, but the appalling existence never touched the hard inner core of this determined survivor. "He gave no thought to the damage these living conditions could inflict on him or anyone else. Nor did he betray even the slightest self-pity at the loss of his entire adolescence. . . . For better or worse he was free of his family's constraints and the world they had imported from Russia, free not only of their demands, but also of their language and religious rituals."

He did his duty by his mother, taking excellent care of her after his father's early death, but he remained emotionally detached from her, and even more, from his brothers and sisters. They, along with their hopelessness, were what he had to shed as he invented Irving Berlin.

Where work was concerned, Izzy the loner could be as sociable as the next fellow. His first friend in the music world was Harry Von Tilzer, composer of "A Bird In a Gilded Cage," who was born Harry Gumm, uncle of Frances Gumm, who later became Judy Garland. Izzy liked the formality and punctiliousness of Von Tilzer's Germanic pseudonym and decided to copy it, signing his first composition "I. Berlin"—a deliberate change, not the printer's error of legend.

As a singing waiter in a raucous watering hole called "Nigger Mike's," Berlin plugged blackface vaudeville numbers called "coon songs," many of them featuring a character named Alexander, which was considered a comical name for a black man in those days. Shrewdly observing that "syncopation is the soul of every American," Berlin began writing songs, turning out a ragtime festival of ethnicity that would cause mass cardiac arrest in our sensitive era: "Sweet Marie, Make-a Rag-a-Time Dance with Me," "Yiddle on Your Fiddle Play Some Ragtime," and one about Harlem fancy-dress balls called "Puttin' on the Ritz" that he sanitized twenty years later by changing Lenox Avenue to Park Avenue.

An untrained musician, he used only the black keys—he called them "nigger keys"—which restricted him to F-sharp. "The key of C is for people who study music," he sneered. With the help of a transposing piano equipped with a key-changing lever like a gear stick, he wrote so many songs so fast that once during a rare lull, another composer wrote "Izzy, Get Busy and Write Another Ragtime Song."

He did. "Alexander's Ragtime Band" in 1910 catapulted him to fame and triggered the rumor that he did not write his songs himself but had a "little nigger boy" who wrote the melodies. "Imagine how many little nigger boys I'd have to have," he retorted. The rumor persisted throughout his career but Laurence Bergreen lays it to rest with convincing insight into Berlin's loner personality: "His desire for control over his songwriting was so great that he was emotionally incapable of entrusting his work to others."

Sexually fastidious—"His morality was a function of his fierce desire for autonomy"—he detested the rutting Florenz Ziegfeld and rejected the many chorus girls at his disposal. In 1912 he married singer Dorothy Goetz, who died five months later of the typhoid she caught on their Cuban honeymoon. In the twelve years before he married again, "he became more inward, not in the sense of becoming introspective, a mental habit he despised, but less trusting of the world around him: his friends, his business partners, even himself."

His first openly misanthropic statement—his coming out, as it were—was the 1914 anti-war fantasy song, "Stay Down Here Where You Belong," in which Satan tells his sons to remain in hell rather than go to war with mankind. It was a flop, but it was quickly forgotten in the glow of success that greeted "Oh, How I Hate to Get Up in the Morning." When his fame approached legendary proportions after World War I, bringing kidnapping threats from anarchists, he wrote "Look Out for That Bolsheviki Man" and bought a bullet-proof limousine.

In 1925 he met the love of his life, debutante Ellin Mackay, daughter of the devoutly Catholic and devoutly anti-Semitic tycoon Clarence Mackay, who lived in a Long Island mansion surrounded by his collection of medieval armor. After a series of Romeo-and-Juliet crises, Irving and Ellin were married at city hall. His wedding present to her was the copyright to "Always," but contrary to legend, he did not write it for her. It was composed originally in 1913 when the girlfriend of a business associate jokingly challenged him to write a song for her on the spot. "I'll Be Loving You, Mona" was never published but Berlin put it in his trunk and reworked the lyrics some years later for a Broadway show.

He was such a loner that he did not even entirely like the idea of being married, and he suffered a composing block for several years after he and Ellin tied the knot. The negative emotions that marriage triggered in him were remarked on by a reporter who saw him on his honeymoon: "The man is in a highly nervous condition. He is a very different person from the suave and debonair Berlin who once strolled down Broadway after dark. That genial smile he had when he and his bride sailed . . . has disappeared. He is . . . morose, irritable, and snaps out the word 'no' when approached by those not bosom friends."

Part of the trouble was Clarence Mackay's refusal to give Ellin his blessing, part of it was the intrusiveness of the press, but even bosom friends like Alexander Woollcott noted that from his second marriage on, Berlin became more "beleagured and belligerent. . . . he could shift to fury without warning, and those who witnessed his behavior inevitably came away with one overriding question: how could the composer of those lovely, sentimental, romantic ballads. . . . suddenly act so crude, glowering and swearing and carrying on as though fate had singled him out for the misfortune of great fame?"

Violinist Fritz Kreisler was shaken by the conversation they had when Berlin tried to buy one of his songs for his music publishing company: "The dreadful language he used was so awful. He began to curse and swear at me."

He also became stingy with money, and even more with permissions, restricting performances of his songs and raising the roof if anyone dared quote even a few words of his lyrics. He treated Ellin the same way, says Bergreen, guarding her "as jealously as he did his songs, and for the same reason: she was all he had. . . . His mentality remained permanently that of the survivor, always vigilant, forever wary of anything beyond his control."

Clarence Mackay eventually came round, more or less, and acknowledged the births of his three granddaughters, but the Berlin home was not a happy one. Ellin had to shield the girls from his rages, and eventually took refuge herself in a late-blooming career as a novelist. Berlin was enthusiastic about her writing when it came to supplying her with publicity ideas, a specialty of his, but when she asked him for the money to buy a new car he snapped, "You've got your own goddamn money."

They became further estranged over politics: he was an arch-conservative and she was a flaming liberal.

His sojourn in Hollywood during the filming of *Holiday Inn* turned into a debacle. Says Bergreen: "Irving remained in a foul temper long after he returned to New York. His outbursts became more intense. . . . They were a highly unattractive but persistent symptom of the impossible demands he made on himself and the corrosive effects of fame on his personality."

When an employee of his music company had a heart attack and asked for an advance on his Christmas bonus to pay his medical bills, the composer of "White Christmas" refused, snarling, "We're not running a charity here." His nephew got the same reception when he asked for money to pay his mother's medical bills. "She's my sister," said Berlin, "but she's your mother. When you use up all your money taking care of her and you run out, then I'll help you out."

He got his comeuppance in 1964 when he lost his suit against *Mad* magazine, which had parodied some of his lyrics. He claimed it was plagiarism because they had used the same meter, but Judge Irving R. Kaufman ruled: "Parody and satire are deserving of substantial freedom both as entertainment and as a form of social and literary criticism. We doubt that even so eminent a composer as Irving Berlin should be permitted to claim a property interest in iambic pentameter."

Irving and Ellin lived in a Beekman Place mansion, but as time went on they did not live together. He had his apartment and she had hers, one upstairs and one down. They met at dinner but he rarely spoke to her or anyone else. On his walks he chased children away and refused to return the greetings of neighbors. His own children and grandchildren never visited; his eruptions of fury had driven them away.

He refused to attend either the Statue of Liberty Centennial, which was built around "God Bless America," or his own centennial birthday party. By then he was virtually blind and completely alone: Ellin, sixteen years his junior, had died in 1988. His own death at the age of 101 came quietly on September 22, 1989.

It seems to me that Laurence Bergreen leans too heavily on the price-of-fame angle to explain Berlin's misanthropy. In our era, the shoe is on the other foot: fans, not celebrities, are the misanthropes among us.

In religious centuries, when everyone from the King down to the most brutish peasant held the same unquestioning belief in the soul's immortality, fame was unimportant, and indeed, did not really exist as we know it today. The common people of France were permitted to wander in and out of Versailles at will and watch the King at his banquet table. He ate in public so that the people could see, not the King, but God's representative on earth. These public displays were in no way comparable to our gaping autograph hunts and photo ops; they were quasi-religious rituals.

When people said excitedly, "I saw the King!" it was not the same as "I saw Liz Taylor!" The latter is always followed by the expression *in person,* but the idea of seeing the King in person would have been a contradiction in terms. It was his spiritual, not his corporeal, presence that mattered.

In today's secular world, celebrities are the only people left who can be certain of attaining the immortality that the humblest medieval serf took for granted. It is the supreme irony of our enlightened democratic age that *in person* is another way of saying that only the famous have souls. The obscure majority are well aware of the New Calvinism and more and more of them are coming to resent it. The shrinking of immortality to a select few whose names will "live" has ushered in a murderous hatred of celebrities that increasingly results in actual murder. Thanks to the New Calvinism, the misanthropic fan is now a fixture of American life.

As for Irving Berlin's misanthropy, I think he was mean because he was mean. So *nu?* I said he bored me, didn't I?

James Gould Cozzens (1903–1978) never used a simple word when an arcane one was available, so nowhere in his rambling analyses of his temperament do we find the word *misanthrope.* He called his condition *inappetency,* a lack of appetite for living. His publisher, who was probably damaged by years of coping with Cozzens's vocabulary, came up with *anhedonia,* an inability to experience pleasure in life. It never seems to have occurred to anyone to try *bastard.*

Cozzens was a professional Wasp in the manner of John O'Hara, except that he really was a Wasp. The only child of a doting mother and a businessman, he grew up on Staten Island, soaked up high-church Episcopalianism at the Kent School, and carried a walking stick in Harvard Yard. "I feel I'm better than other people," he told *Time* years later.

He did not graduate from Harvard because he had run up so many bills that he could not afford to join Porcellian, and death being preferable to not joining Porcellian, he quit college after his second year.

His first novel, published in 1924, was the well-titled *Confusion,* obviously inspired by F. Scott Fitzgerald's *This Side of Paradise,* about a young man on the brink of life, or the edge of the abyss, or something: the frat rat as Stella Dallas. Five more novels followed; none of them sold well but Cozzens did not have to worry. He had married Bernice Baumgarten, a crackerjack literary agent who supported him. "It could have been a humiliating situation," he told *Time,* "but I guess I had a certain native conceit and felt that her time was well spent."

Guard of Honor, about racial segregation in the World War II army, won the 1949 Pulitzer Prize, but even it did not sell really well. After that came a silence of eight years: Cozzens was busy writing his masterpiece, *By Love Possessed,* published in 1957.

It covers two days in the life of a repressed, eminently respectable Wasp lawyer whose carefully controlled existence is shattered by a rape case, an embezzling partner, a cuckolded partner, an hysterical woman in the throes of conversion to Catholicism, and painful memories triggered by all of the above.

The critics greeted *By Love Possessed* with orgasmic delight. Never, before or since, have so many people typed c-o-m-p-e-l-l-i-n-g so many times in the course of a single season. All the Lit Crit big guns, from Orville Prescott to Jessamyn West, called the novel spellbinding and enchanting, wise and compassionate, distinguished and truly distinguished, as well as magnificent, utterly magnificent, and simply magnificent. Finally, one critic simply gave up and wrote, "about all I can do is ditto the dithyrambs."

Taking note of this blizzard of superlatives, the major book clubs and *Reader's Digest* joined the parade, until *By Love Possessed,* all 570 pages of it, squatted on maple-veneer Early American coffee tables throughout the land. When it drove *Peyton Place* out of the top slot on the lists, Hollywood perked up and completed the cycle of success.

There was only one thing wrong with *By Love Possessed,* but none of the critics wanted to be the first to say what it was. It's dangerous to go against the grain of opinion, especially when the grain comes from the paneled dens of the country's best ivory towers, wherein dwell the kind of people who can't bear to admit that they don't understand something. And if the exalted Lit Crits would not speak out, the matrons of Dubuque certainly were not about to. Instead, they sat on their Early American sofas with Cozzens in their laps, hating themselves for being too stupid and provincial to appreciate what they were reading:

> The sweeping voiceless compliment, the silent, single-minded expression of so real a respect (surely real, being silent, being supposed private) could not but gratify; yet, to most people, pause must also be brought—pause, both on one's own behalf (to protest self-consciously: not so! would be a gross gawkishness; while the grave acceptance of no comment must amount to, be the next thing to, the nod complacent, to oneself proclaiming: *I am not as other men are, extortioners, unjust adulterers . . .);* and on behalf of the single-minded complimenter (not a high look only, but a high aspiration, is apt to go before a fall).

Out of context, you say? Okey-dokey, let's try another one:

> Ah, how wise, how sure, how right, was that genius of the language whose instinct detected in the manifold manifestings of the amative appetite (however different-seeming; however apparently opposed) the one same urgent unreason, the one same eager let's-pretend, and so, wisely consented, so, for convenience covenanted, to name all with one same name! Explaining, sweet unreason excused; excusing, sweet let's-pretend explained. The young heart, indentured (O wearisome conditions of humanity!) to reason, pined, starved on the bare bitter diet of thinking. One fine day, that heart (most hearts) must bolt. That heart would be off (could you blame it?) to Loveland, to feeling's feasts.

There *must* be something without parentheses, you say? You're right, there is:

> Deaf as yesterday to all representations of right, he purposed further perfidy, once more pawning his honor to obtain his lust.

Deaf as yesterday to all remonstrances of reason, he purposed to sell himself over again to buy venery's disappearing dross.

You won't believe me until you see the sexy parts, will you? Jessamyn West said they had "lyric power." Maybe she meant: "the thoroughgoing, deepening, widening work of their connection; and his then no less than hers, the tempo slowed in concert to engineer a tremulous joint containment and continuance."

Some of the Lit Crits mentioned in passing that Cozzens's style was a little hard to follow, but then quickly added that the same was true of Henry James and William Faulkner, thereby elevating Cozzens still higher. The fraud was finally exposed by Dwight MacDonald, who reviewed the reviewers in a devastating *Commentary* piece, "By Cozzens Possessed," in which he said that the sex scene so admired by Jessamyn West read like "a *Fortune* description of an industrial process." He also accused Cozzens of making "a dead style even deader" with negative constructions like "not-unhelped" and "unhasty," said he had a tin ear for speech, and wrote prose "as Gothic as Harkness Memorial Quadrangle. . . . Haven't seen 'dross' in print since *East Lynne.*"

The most puzzling aspect of *By Love Possessed* is that Cozzens had not written this way before. His earlier novels were couched in what MacDonald called "a straightforward if commonplace style." But because he was "slimly endowed as either thinker or stylist, he has succeeded only in fuzzing it up, inverting the syntax, dragging in Latin-root polysyllables. . . . Like shot in game or sand in clams, such gritty nuggets are strewn through the book *to set on edge the teeth of the reader. . . .*"

My italics. I maintain that Cozzens wrote *By Love Possessed* in this turgid manner not out of creative experimentation or any other literary reason, but as a deliberate and conscious attempt to be user-unfriendly. By this time he was virtually a hermit who never left his home deep in the New Jersey sticks (Bernice had to endure a complicated train trip to New York each day). Unable to stand eating in restaurants unless the nearby tables were unoccupied, compelled to wear gloves year-round to ward off the taint of his fellow man, he made his torturous literary style the final manifestation of his misanthropy. He wanted to make his readers suffer, and if possible, drive the entire country blind and crazy.

Unlike his fiction, Cozzens's journal entries are coherent and valuable for their unvarnished view of mankind. The millions who are presently fiddling with self-esteem while America burns would do well to examine this one:

> The seamy side of human nature. You must be careful how you treat people as your equals. The average person has much more respect for you if, even though he resents it, you make it plain to him that you consider him of no great importance. The line may be a thin one, but if you're 'nice' to him beyond what he, perhaps subconsciously, feels are his deserts he will much more often than not despise you for it.

I have found this to be true. Insecurity breeds treachery: if you are kind to people who hate themselves, they will hate you as well. It does no good to try to help them because they never really change no matter how long they stay in therapy. Even so progressive a spirit as Isadora Duncan admitted as much when she wrote: "It is only in romances that people undergo a sudden metamorphosis. In real life, the main character remains exactly the same."

Insecure people are dangerous and it is best to stay away from them. Especially now, when there are so many of them, only a misanthrope can avoid being exsanguinated by their emotional demands. The mere sonofabitch, in saner times an automatic survivor, has fallen upon hard times and is currently in grave peril.

Cozzens's boorishness was legendary. Like everyone without a sense of humor, he thought he had one. Attending a dinner for his wife's bestselling client Betty MacDonald, he ridiculed *The Egg and I* until he had the author in tears.

His publicly expressed attitude toward his wife defies belief. Describing his feelings on first meeting her, he told *Time:* "I suppose sex entered into it. After all, what's a woman for?" Of his decision to marry: "Mother almost died when I married a Jew, but later when she saw I was being decently cared for, she realized that it was the best thing that could have happened to me."

Both of these remarks pale beside a story told by Cozzens biographer Matthew J. Bruccoli: "They did not want children. Neither one was philoprogenitive, and Cozzens later remarked that he didn't want a son of his kept out of Porcellian because he was half Jewish. Bernice had an abortion when she became pregnant."

I wish there were some way to keep Cozzens out of Misanthropian. He wasn't really one of us at all, merely a mean drunk at the country club.

THE OLD MISANTHROPE

My favorite misanthrope, Ambrose Bierce (1842–1914?), would spin in his grave, wherever it is, if he knew what Hollywood did to him.

In *The Old Gringo,* Bierce is portrayed as a sentimental idealist by Gregory Peck, America's Nice Guy Next Door: Earnest Division, who gave his humanitarian all in the successful campaign to keep Robert Bork off the Supreme Court.

The real Ambrose Bierce, according to a friendly biographer, believed that the Fifth Amendment should be replaced with the medieval trial by ordeal: "Any pressure short of physical torture or the threat of it, that can be put upon a rogue to make him assist in his own undoing is just and therefore expedient."

The Old Gringo was based on the novel by Mexican socialist Carlos Fuentes. The real old gringo wrote: "No people in the world are fit for Socialism. I don't believe in the greatest good to the greatest number. It seems to me perfect rot. I believe in the greatest good to the best men. And I would sacrifice a hundred incapable men to elevate one really great man."

Jane Fonda, a friend of Carlos Fuentes, stars in the movie as a woman who inspired love and trust in the heart of the fictional old gringo, notwithstanding the sentiments that spewed regularly from the real old gringo's pen: "There is positively no betting on the discreet reticence of any woman whose silence you have not secured with a meat-ax. . . . The mind that cannot discern a score of great and irreparable general evils distinctly traceable to 'emancipation of women' is as impregnable to the light as a toad in a rock."

Ambrose Bierce was born on the Ohio frontier, which he hated, and later moved with his family to the Indiana frontier, which he also hated. The sentimental glorification of frontier boyhood in Hamlin Garland's *Son of the Middle Border* inspired him to write a poem about the sun's refraction off the henhouse slime and the maggoty straw on the warped floorboards of the sheep cote.

There were eight little Bierces, all of them given names beginning with *A* by a father who never explained this idiosyncrasy. Ambrose rather liked his father, with whom he shared a taste for reading, but he disdained his mother and all his siblings except his brother Albert, whom he tolerated to the extent of letting him come along on solitary walks through the woods.

Bierce, who was later to define misanthropy as "a hatred of youth and of being young," felt the same way about childhood as Ayn Rand: he was against it. Barbara Branden's comments on this aspect of Rand—"Childhood was an overture, she concluded, a preparation for the future, with no significance in itself"—match those of Bierce's biographer, Richard O'Connor: "Youth, it seemed to him, was something to be gotten over as quickly as possible, with adulthood the only goal worthwhile."

161

These attitudes recall Jonathan Swift's maxim: "No wise man ever wished to be younger." It was not simply that Rand and Bierce came as adults to dislike children (they did), but that they disliked children while they were children themselves, and resented *being* children. I know the feeling well; it's hard to be a misanthrope when you're that short.

As far as anyone could see, the man who would one day be called "Bitter Bierce" had nothing to be bitter about. He was an Adonis, with thick, curly golden hair, piercing blue eyes, and a perfect physique that was enhanced by the uniform of the Ninth Indiana when the eighteen-year-old Bierce answered Lincoln's call for volunteers in 1861.

Biographer Richard O'Connor believes "repressed idealism" made him rally so quickly to the colors. It certainly was not patriotism in the standard sense; his taste for irreverent verse inspired him to write:

> My country 'tis of thee, sweet land of felony,
> Of thee I sing.
> Land where my fathers fried young witches
> And applied whips to the Quaker's hide
> And made him spring.

Anyone who replaces belief in God with belief in the human comedy ("Death is not the end, there remains litigation over the estate") tends to develop the kind of panache that leads to great courage. Bierce was wounded twice, decorated for valor twelve times, and received a battlefield commission at Shiloh, eventually rising to the rank of brevet major.

Later on, during the post-war "Gilded Age" of greed and political scandals, he was to write: "It was once my fortune to command a company of soldiers—real soldiers. Not professional life-long fighters, the product of European militarism—just plain, ordinary, American, volunteer soldiers who loved their country and fought for it with never a thought of grabbing it for themselves; that is a trick which the survivors were taught later by gentlemen desiring their votes."

War suited him perfectly. Had he been less intelligent, the carnage he witnessed combined with his bleak opinion of humankind would have pushed him over the edge into sadism. As it was, the horrors of war generated a gallows humor and a macabre joie de vivre that pervade his writing, from the definitions in *The Devil's Dictionary* (*"non-combatant:* A dead Quaker") to his short stories.

An early critic predicted that Bierce's work would "never achieve a wide popularity, at least among the Anglo-Saxon race. His writings have too much the flavour of the hospital and the morgue. There is a stale odour of mouldy cerements about them." In *Patriotic Gore,* a study of Civil War literature, Edmund Wilson compared Bierce's writing to his asthma—"an art that can hardly breathe"—and attributed both to psychological causes. Clifton Fadiman acknowledged the morbidity but deemed it non-neurotic: "It merely expresses his fury at our placid healthfulness."

Bierce's fictional objective follows his own maxim: "A jest in the death chamber startles by surprise." We don't want to laugh when the sentry discovers that he shot his own father, or when the Yankee twin turns over a Confederate corpse and looks down at his own face, yet Bierce deadpans his climaxes in such a way that the reader's mind flashes a picture of Peter Sellers as Inspector Clouseau surveying another inadvertency.

To all who criticized his sepulchral bent Bierce replied: "If it scares you to read about one imaginary person killing another, why not take up knitting?"

After the war he worked briefly as a Treasury agent assigned to confiscate Rebel property in Selma, Alabama. Blood and guts on the battlefield hadn't bothered him at all, but witnessing the wholesale plunder carried out by the Reconstruction government offended his rigid sense of honor so much that he came out against peace: "I favor war, famine, pestilence—anything that will stop the people from cheating and confine the practice to contractors and statesmen."

He went to San Francisco and got a job on Hearst's newspaper, *The Examiner,* where he wrote his famous one-sentence book review: "The covers of this book are too far apart." His idealism was soon placed on the line again when he exposed the financial shenanigans of the Southern Pacific Railroad, and Colis P. Huntington tried to buy him off. "Name your price," said Huntington, "every man has a price." Bierce roared: "The price is about seventy-five million dollars, to be handed to the Treasurer of the United States!"

His daily column, "Prattle," became a catalogue of his likes and dislikes. The former included Jews and Chinese, and also Mormons, whom he embraced out of contrariness from having seen them persecuted during his Indiana boyhood. A critic, journalist, and writer himself, he nonetheless hated critics, journalists, and writers—when Jack London was lost at sea Bierce predicted, "The ocean will refuse to swallow him." He hated all sports and said that athletes moved him to "the lofty compassion of an owl for a blind puppy in a dark cellar." Dwight Moody and other evangelists were a "he-harlotry of horribles" and "phylloxera of the moral vineyard."

His hatreds included all "isms" but he readily admitted that laissez-faire capitalism's emphasis on freedom of action encouraged people to behave in ways that provided grist for his misanthrope's mill. Also: labor organizers, socialists, social workers (a misanthropic favorite), teachers, scientists, doctors, lodge members, dishonest people, religious people, and above all, the unintelligent. "That left him a very narrow segment of the population of whom he could approve, a fact which did not dismay him in the least," writes O'Connor.

Above all, he hated women. The three exceptions were George Eliot, the Empress Eugénie of France, and Lillie Coit, a San Francisco eccentric who rode to fires on the back of fire engines. "Lil is a real woman," he said fondly. He admired novelist Gertrude Atherton for her masculine drive and ambition but condemned her spready, run-on literary style as hopelessly feminine—though neither quality stopped him from making a pass at her as they waited for a train.

The rest of womankind were impeded by "the gray batter of their brainettes." Unlike most misogynists, he did not even credit female intuition for occasionally being right for the wrong reasons. "A woman does not leap to correct conclusions," he wrote. "Her saltatory feats commonly land her in a bog. . . . To put the matter with entire lucidity, woman hasn't any thinker." Opinions like these made radical feminist Charlotte Perkins Gilman call him a "public tormentor."

All women got on his nerves but one in particular drove him up the wall: "A sweetheart is a bottle of wine; a wife is a wine bottle." Mollie Day Bierce was the sort of cheerful soft-hearted woman guaranteed to rouse his contempt, which may have been why he married her. Misanthropes can't resist tormenting such people; I once had an affair with a man because he said, "The best thing about a beautiful spring day is being able to share it with someone else." I had to get at him.

Ambrose and Mollie had a daughter and two sons, both of the latter born in London where the Bierces lived for several years while Ambrose worked on a British journal, *The Lantern.* The children got on his nerves. "It's all a gyp perpetrated by women," he said. "Only a fool feels any lasting pride of fatherhood." Refusing to be domesticated, he came and went as he pleased. Although he said, "May Heaven punish the malefactor who invented that deadly dull thing, a good time," he enjoyed staying out late and drinking with his literary confrères, which meant that the only times he saw his family were when he was nursing a hangover. It was on one of these occasions that he lectured his son on blasphemy when he heard the boy say "Damn God." Bierce snapped: "I have told you repeatedly never to say Damn God when you mean goddamn."

The marriage broke up when Bierce found some innocuous letters addressed to Mollie from a platonic male friend. Refusing to listen to her protests of innocence, which several family friends verified, Bierce walked out then and there and never lived with her again. Several commentators have attributed this precipitous action to touchy pride or common-garden jealousy, but it's clear to me that Bierce simply latched onto the letters as an excuse to leave her. To a misanthrope, a sexual relationship is the grand-daddy of Reach Out and Touch Someone, a literal rendition of "Peepul Who Need Peepul," the navel as Smile Button. When the resentment of intimacy mounts and the urge to circle the Welcome Wagons comes over us, we frequently turn against our sexual partners as symbols of an activity that, when you think about it, is life's oldest form of teamwork.

Bierce's older son died in a duel. The younger one married a girl his father disapproved of, giving Bierce a perfect excuse not to see him again. When this son committed suicide, Bierce kept his cremated remains in a cigar box on his desk.

Only his daughter Helen remained, and she knew something was up when Bierce visited her in the summer of 1913 with his literary papers in tow and asked her to store them for him. He was going to Mexico, ostensibly as an observer of the Pancho Villa revolution, but his famous rhetorical question—"Why should I remain in a country that is on the verge of Prohibition and Women's Suffrage?"—hints that he did not plan to return to the United States. More telling are his remarks in a letter to his niece: "If you hear of my being stood up against a Mexican stone wall and shot to rags, please know that I think that a pretty good way to depart this life. It beats old age, disease or falling down the cellar stairs. To be a Gringo in Mexico—ah, that is euthanasia!"

Another letter he wrote that summer was typical of a misanthrope saying goodbye to someone he cares for. It was addressed to his brother Albert, the only sibling he ever liked, and it was so violent and abusive that Albert was never the same after reading it. Five months later, after a debilitating bout with insomnia, Albert died of a stroke. Edmund Wilson, who was no bundle of sweetness 'n' light himself, went unerringly to the heart of the matter when he suggested that the letter "may have been Bierce's strange way of trying to diminish the grief that he knew the affectionate Albert would feel at the news of his death."

Bierce presumably died, though not necessarily by execution, in the Mexican revolution. We don't know; his trail dried up suddenly, and no one could be found who had seen the unmistakable gringo, still handsome and impressive at seventy-one. Richard O'Connor speculates that he might have made his way down through Central America and thence into the wilds of the Andes, there to live out his life as a solitary hermit on a mountaintop, chuckling gleefully at the thought of the many search parties combing Mexico for him or his bones. I would like to think that this is what happened.

Whatever happened, his object was to get away from America, which he had come to loathe for its democracy and equality, believing they foretold "the doom of authority." He advocated strong control over the masses, the churches, public meetings, telegraph, and railroads. As for anarchists who committed acts of violence, the proper punishment was "mutilation followed by death."

Living in a blunter age, he did not have to defend his turf via the genteel circuitous route of mailing a check for thirty dollars to U. S. English. "The American eagle has become a buzzard," he announced. "It is the immigration of 'the oppressed of all nations' that has made this country one of the worst on the face of the earth. . . . as always and everywhere, the oppressed are unworthy of asylum, avenging upon those who gave them sanctuary the wrongs from which they fled. The saddest thing about oppression is that it makes its victims unfit for anything but to be oppressed. . . . In the end they turn out to be fairly energetic oppressors themselves."

He looked favorably on eugenics as a way of improving the citizenry—"I think it's very strange that you people who recognize the differences in horses and dogs don't recognize the differences in the human race"—and although he claimed to hate monarchies, he gave them the nod in the area of cultural excellence: "It is the despotisms of the world that have been the conservators of civilization."

Comparing Bierce's reaction against democracy to that of the later Mark Twain, Edmund Wilson wrote: "The insistence of Ambrose Bierce on discipline, law and order, and on the need for the control of the disorderly mob by an enlightened and well-washed minority has today a familiar fascistic ring."

True enough, but the left-wing Wilson forgot to include his own side. Socialists have their own agenda for discipline and law and order, and they also believe in the control of the disorderly mob by an enlightened, though not necessarily well-washed, minority. Extremists right and left are cut out of the same piece of cloth. Both are idealists with lofty standards for human nature who often become misanthropic once the inevitable disillusionment sets in. Right wingers, concluding that mankind is despicable and hopeless, turn to the savage misanthropy of Jonathan Swift and Ambrose Bierce. Left wingers, concluding that mankind is inherently good and needs only one more chance to prove it, turn to the sentimental misanthropy of Jean-Jacques Rousseau and his naive dream of universal love and cooperation. Both are susceptible to totalitarianism, for when human nature invariably declines to be perfected, the only thing left to perfect is the State.

Writing on Ambrose Bierce in the late 1940s, Clifton Fadiman suggested that "the purity of his misanthropy" might one day "speak to us with added vehemence" in some future era of pessimism when an America hungry for leadership had come to hate those "in the saddle." Richard O'Connor echoes the same thought: "He may still be regarded in the future, if it should develop as he foresaw into an anarchic nightmare, as something more than a minor prophet, a disgruntled voice in the wilderness."

We could do a lot worse than Ambrose Bierce. H.L. Mencken accused him of being "quite unable to imagine the heroic, in any ordinary sense," but that more accurately describes Mencken himself. Bierce's credo, delivered as advice to the readers of his column, is a prescription for ordinary everyday heroism that ought to be adopted as the official oath of office in the Republic of Nice:

> Be as decent as you can. Don't believe without evidence. Treat things divine with marked respect—and don't have anything to do with them. Do not trust humanity without collateral security;

it will play you some scurvy trick. Remember that it hurts no one to be treated as an enemy entitled to respect until he shall prove himself a friend worthy of affection. Cultivate a taste for distasteful truths. And, finally, most important of all, endeavor to see things as they are, not as they ought to be.

Always depend upon the kindness of misanthropes.

THE MOTHER OF
ALL ATTITUDES

What is it like being a misanthrope on a daily basis? Much depends upon the kind of people you encounter. Generally speaking, they fall into two categories: those who know what the word means and those who don't.

The former always ask the same question in properly shocked American tones.

"How can you hate *people*?"

"Who else is there to hate?"

The others are like the persistent president of a Southern women's club that wanted to take a literary tour of Europe and offered me a free trip in exchange for being their guide. I put her off politely the first two times she called, but the third time I decided to be blunt.

"I can't, I'm a misanthrope."

"Oh, honey, you don't have to let it cramp your style! My sister-in-law's a diabetic and she can go anywhere she wants as long as she takes her little kit with her."

FLORENCE KING

My debut as a misanthrope occurred shortly after I learned to talk. I was being wheeled through a store in my stroller when a child-loving woman exclaimed, "What a darling little girl!" and squatted down in front of me.

"Hello, you sweet thing," she cooed.

"I doan yike you," I replied.

Thereafter I latched onto the sentence as children will, and said it to every stranger who crossed my path. My extroverted grandmother always hastened to explain, "She's just shy"— America's favorite rationalization for misanthropy and one which I was destined to hear time and time again over the years.

America's second favorite rationalization for misanthropy is, "She's been deeply hurt," often pieced out for greater adverbial effect with "somewhere, sometime, by someone." I often get this from reviewers who, as citizens of the Republic of Nice, feel guilty about liking my books. A male reviewer, after placing me "in the first rank of American wits," added: "But like Dorothy Parker, King's success might well have been purchased with the coin of personal happiness."

Female reviewers are even more determined to find hidden tragedy. Said one: "Despite the wisdom and clear, clever observations King makes, the reader can't help but wonder if this woman's acid wit is the result of a lifelong feeling of rejection cushioned by books, which, if true, is very sad."

America's third rationalization for misanthropy is, "Oh, you're just kidding." It goes like this:

"Why don't you go on the 'Today Show'?"

"I'd rather corner them in a dungeon and pull the caps off their teeth. The only thing I have in common with those people is a sofa."

"Oh, you're just kidding."

Oh, no I'm not. The person I admire above all others is the

man who died on the "Dick Cavett Show." I forget his name but it doesn't matter; to a veteran of book-promotion tours who has walked through the valley of the shadow of Happy Talk, he will go down in history as the Man Who Got Even. Having no wish to emulate him, however, I told my publisher that I am through touring books. I went to college with Willard Scott so I was already half dead in 1955, and I have no intention of letting him and his ilk finish me off now.

The American misanthrope who writes has an especially hard row to hoe. Unflagging optimism has been our chief characteristic as a people from the beginning, and our writers have been throwing up their hands in despair ever since. Herman Melville bewailed "the everlasting Yea"; H.L. Mencken spoke scathingly of "the heaven-kissing heroes of the $1.08 counter"; and James M. Cain deplored "the curse of American literature—the sympathetic character."

My own nemesis is the word *upbeat,* used constantly by an editor I once worked with. The most relentlessly cheerful person I have ever met, he seemed to take my temperament as a personal challenge. During the course of our project he enclosed a "Love Is . . ." cartoon in every letter. He also sent me a Norman Cousins roundup; a profile of Marjorie Holmes; a syndicated filler called "Heartstrings"; and a *National Enquirer* clipping about a poll that found that the most popular television shows were those on which married couples sang love songs to each other.

As things turned out, the novel I wrote for him was never published, possibly because I finally told him that if he had been the editor on *Anna Karenina,* he would have said, "Leo, please, take out the train."

The luck of misanthropy is in the chronological draw. History must contain some dawn when bliss it was to be a misanthrope, but I missed it. Instead, I landed in the Age of the Darling Little Girl.

When I was born in 1936, Shirley Temple was at the height of her fame. When I was seven there was Margaret O'Brien, and just as I entered my teens, along came Debbie Reynolds. Between O'Brien and Reynolds there was someone else as well. "Why can't you be sweet and nice like June Allyson?" Granny whispered beside me in the dark. This went on for several years, until Allyson starred as the castrating wife in *The Shrike.*

In view of the misanthrope's icy contempt for helpers and healers, I doubt if psychiatric literature contains any case histories of misanthropy per se. There exists, however, a small amount of material on an aberration connected to misanthropy. Known colloquially as "itchy feet," its clinical name is *dromomania,* from the Greek *dromos,* "to run," and I've had it for years.

Although I hate to travel, I love to move. As a child I collected road maps and gazed contentedly at them by the hour, sounding out the names of strange new places and wondering what it would be like to live in them. When I grew up I did something about it. Since graduating from college I have had some forty addresses in various parts of the country, most for a few months and none for more than three years, until moving to my present apartment, where I have lived for eight years.

The link between misanthropy and dromomania is pinpointed by Kathleen Winsor in her second novel, *Star Money:*

What a relief it was to have anything done, finished, over with for good. So you could throw it out of your life and forget it and go on to something new. Some of her happiest moments had been spent cleaning out closets or drawers, throwing things away, knowing that whatever the symbolism they had had for her, she was destroying it. Each time she finished with something or someone and knew that she had finished forever, it gave her in some sense the illusion of having been granted a new beginning to life. . . .

For some time now I have been planning to move to the mountains of western Virginia. My object is to live in a place that does not call itself "the community with a heart." I want one of those godforsaken towns where all the young people leave and the rest sit on the porch with a rifle across their knees.

I would have moved by now but I had to wait for the 1991 Census figures to find out which towns are losing population; then I got involved in this book and didn't want to move in the middle of it. Meanwhile, to make myself feel that I was doing something to hasten the day, I cleaned out my closets and drawers with the same absorbing pleasure described by Kathleen Winsor. (Clutter symbolizes a life filled with people so misanthropes tend to be excellent housekeepers.)

When I finished, my apartment looked like a Spartan barracks, but the mood was still on me, so I had the back seat taken out of my car.

Ostensibly, it was to make more packing space, but subconsciously I did it for the sheer thrill of shedding something else. After the surgery, when I looked back at all that beautiful emptiness (I'm an agora*phili*ac), I was overcome by an irresistible impulse to have the buddy seat taken out as well.

I reasoned that I've had only two passengers in ten years, so I really don't need it; moreover, I'm so used to driving alone that it makes me nervous to have someone else with me. Best of all, a car with nothing but a driver's seat would be a bona fide misanthrope's car. The only trouble was, other people might not see it that way. The cops might pull me over and ask me what I was planning to transport, and if I should move to another state and have to take another driving test, where would the examiner sit?

I didn't do it.

By all rights, a misanthrope should be a Luddite. Being in favor of advanced technology is a progressive stance, and progressive people are full of genial beans and high hopes for mankind. But technology is also "cold," and therein lies its charm for me.

In one of my battles with local feminists in the letters column of the long-suffering *Free Lance-Star,* the president of Fredericksburg NOW latched onto an article of mine in *MS.* in which I said that I had fallen in love with my computer. Taking it literally as feminists will, she wrote: "Erich Fromm described the most disturbing and extreme form of necrophilia as a fascination for machines rather than people. Can this explain Flo?"

When will feminists learn to think before they write? The most disturbing and extreme form of necrophilia is *necrophilia.* Be that as it may, the NOW cow belled me accurately.

After vowing initially that I would never give up my typewriter; that, indeed, I would use a quill or even a stone tablet and a chisel rather than yield to "word processing," I was forced to buy a computer when a reviewing contract with *Newsday* stipulated that I had to send in my copy via modem. My new "system" was delivered on the day of the 1987 stock market crash. Computers were being blamed for the calamity so I began to think better of them, and by the end of the first week I was hooked. I realize that describing something as being "better than sex" has all the stylistic grace of a Levi's Cotton Dockers commercial, but it's true.

I now feel the same way about my new fax machine. The fax is a boon to civilization and Western culture because it helps misanthropes do what we do best: keep the epistolary art alive.

A letter is affection at a distance and a fax gets it there quicker, combining the joy of letterwriting with the speed of phoning, and leaving a record that would otherwise vanish into the sound waves. Thanks to faxing, I can savor the warmth of communication and human contact without leaving the house or talking to a soul. I can even practice my version of Southern hospitality: standing in front of the machine and watching the paper appear over the edge is like standing at the window watching for company, except I don't say "Oh, God, here they come."

Now that high tech has created the growing trend of working at home, the day of the misanthrope is fast approaching. The usual bevy of psychological counselors has sprung up to advise newly minted homeworkers on how to "answer the needs" of family members who "place demands" upon the worker's time and persist in "invading his space." Suggestions abound, including drawing little pictures of computers on the children's calendar, but the handwriting is already on the wall, right up there with the children's crayon scrawls.

Although the counselors will never admit it, the best way to handle invading family members is not to have any in the first place. In lieu of that, you must feel comfortable practicing the dying art of yelling "goddamnit!" But these solutions are *inappropriate,* so most attempts to work at home will founder on the shoals of the Republic of Nice, leaving the way open for misanthropes to corner the market.

Misanthropes have some admirable if paradoxical virtues. It is no exaggeration to say that we are among the nicest people you are likely to meet. Because good manners build sturdy walls, our distaste for intimacy makes us exceedingly cordial "ships that pass in the night." As long as you remain a stranger we will be your friend forever.

We are law-abiding to the point of punctiliousness, not because we are plaster saints, but because criminals must deal with people constantly. Most crimes require a gift of gab and an ability to inspire trust in the victim, so misanthropes do not become con artists. We do not take hostages because once you have them you can't let them out of your sight. We do not commit serial murder because we recoil in moral revulsion at the very word: *serial*. As for child molestation, in order to molest a child you must first be in the same room with a child, and I don't know how perverts stand it.

We are America's last Spartans, for next to the communality of crime is the freemasonry of illness. We ignore pain because our worst nightmare is being in a hospital and coming to the attention of volunteer strokers who serenade us with "You'll Never Walk Alone."

Misanthropes set a valuable example, or at least offer a change of pace, for youth-obsessed America: we don't like being young.

In *The Palace Guard,* Dan Rather and Gary Paul Gates write that Richard Nixon's "deep-in-the-gut loathing for the sixties" was not only political but "an integral part of his personality." Where other politicians strive for an image of eternal youth, say the authors, Nixon did the opposite:

As a young Congressman, Nixon gave the impression of being older than he was—a man, say, in his middle to late forties. In an eerie sort of way, he has remained frozen in that bracket into his sixties, as though he had made some kind of Faustian bargain to give up the spark of youth in exchange for becoming forever forty-seven.

I think I must have sensed this about Nixon years ago. During his vice-presidency, when I was in college and everyone was saying "There's something about that man I don't like," there was something about him that I *did* like, though I couldn't put my finger on it. As time went on I realized that it was empathy. Like Nixon, I was born to be middle-aged, and now I am.

Ambrose Bierce's definition of misanthropy, "a hatred of youth and of being young," explains much about my earlier life. I no longer drink the way I used to. There hasn't been a bottle of hard liquor in the house for several years now. I didn't try to stop drinking; the craving just petered out gradually, very much the way my menstruation did, and over the same period of time.

I'll still take a drink if somebody offers me one in a social situation, but if you have read this far you know that such situations don't arise very often. Now I have an occasional beer while watching baseball, and burgundy with Italian food, and that's it. Now that my youth is gone I have no more sorrows to drown and no more conflicts to deaden. My temperament and my age are a matched set at last; I like being over the hill.

I expect old age to suit me even better because there is so much more leeway. The younger a misanthrope is, the less he—and especially she—can get away with. I long ago learned that no young woman can be an eccentric; people simply will not accept it. Oblique behavior and outlandish statements from a woman of twenty or thirty are greeted with speechless fury, but when she does and says the same things fifty years later, everyone smiles indulgently and says, "Oh, well, she's old."

My day is coming, and my model is a character in Henry Cecil's novel, *Daughters in Law*.

Miss Pringle, a misanthropic spinster and gardening author *(Weeds Are My Business),* decides to make her Will. Knowing that she eats the unwary for breakfast, her long-suffering solicitors send her the tyro they have just hired and sit back to see what happens.

Miss Pringle begins by telling the young lawyer that she has no one to leave her money to; no relatives, and no friends either, because she's a recluse.

"It isn't that I mind people so much—they're all right so long as they don't talk. It's then I can't stand them."

She pauses a moment to let the lawyer digest this, then proceeds to dictate the strategy she has devised.

"Take this down. I leave nothing to no one. I know the grammar's bad, but it has rather a pleasant sound about it."

Explaining that this will only deliver her estate into the hands of the government, which she hates, the lawyer suggests that she leave her money to a charity.

Miss Pringle: "There oughtn't to be any charities."

Lawyer: "Some deserving person—an artist or an actor or an author who needs help to keep going?"

Miss Pringle: "What do you mean by deserving? People deserve what they get and get what they deserve. If you give an artist enough to live on he gets lazy."

The lawyer suggests the church.

Miss Pringle: "The church has gone into business."

Lawyer: Animal welfare?

Miss Pringle: "Then they'd say I was potty. Left all her money to a cats' home. I know how they talk."

The lawyer suggests sports, "such as cricket, tennis, or football."

Miss Pringle: "D'you call that sport? No one kills anything."

Lawyer: Research?

Miss Pringle: "There's too much research. People are too inquisitive."

Desperate now, the lawyer suggests nuclear weapons—meaning a peace movement, but Miss Pringle interprets it in her own way.

"For two thousand years we've been preaching peace through

love and a nice mess we've made of it. But peace through fear is better than no peace at all. And, as long as both sides have enough weapons to blow the other side's blooming heads off, they won't use them."

So Miss Pringle leaves her money in trust for the creation of bigger and better bombs.

To answer the question that I am frequently asked: No, I don't worry about "dying alone." There is, after all, no other way to die. We come into the world alone and we leave it alone, regardless of how many presumptive loved ones are clustered around our bed. Even in a suicide pact, as Crown Prince Rudolph must have realized to his dismay on that iron January dawn at Mayerling, someone must go first.

I do worry about dying alone—without the quotation marks. I live alone and intend to keep on living alone, so chances are I'll die at home and nobody will know until somebody in New York starts wondering why they haven't heard from me.

It's an unfastidious thought but if it must be, then so be it. I'd rather rot on my own floor than be found by a bunch of bingo players in a nursing home.

EPILOGUE:
A MISANTHROPE'S
GARDEN OF VERSES

Jonathan Odell may be America's most obscure misanthrope. Born into an old established colonial Puritan family, he began life as an army doctor and served in the King's forces in the West Indies.

And then something came over him. Today we would call it Anglophilia, but in Odell's time there was no Alistair Cooke to give it a good name by sitting down in a leather chair and crossing his legs as legs have never been crossed before. In the 1770s it was called Toryism, and Odell became its most implacable purveyor.

He gave up medicine and went to London to study for the Anglican priesthood. After his ordination he returned to the American colonies and set about the daunting task of persuading New England Congregationalists to take the wine. They didn't, but a group of British officers did. They took quite a bit of it on June 4, 1776, during a rousing celebration of the King's birthday hosted by Odell and highlighted by the singing of a song he wrote in honor of George III.

Wakened by the drunken roars pouring out of the rectory in the middle of the night, the local patriots listened to the lyrics and decided that Odell had to go. Escaping one step ahead of the lynch mob, he took refuge behind British lines, serving as a courier in the Benedict Arnold affair and turning out Tory poetry in his spare time.

Odell's writings consist of four satires in verse written between 1779 and 1780. In the preface to one of them he signals the reader what to expect by decreeing that "Ridicule may lawfully be employed in the Service of Virtue." The time had come to do so, he went on, because he had tried everything else he could think of to convince the erring rebels of their duty to their King. He, along with a few other enlightened thinkers, had *explained* why revolution was wrong, but nobody would *listen,* so what else could he *do* but write nasty poetry? "Reason has done her part, and therefore this is the legitimate moment for Satire."

The satire did not come off because the tightly wound Odell had worked himself into such a snit that by the time he took up his pen, he had lost what little sense of humor he might once have possessed.

Worse, he took himself seriously. "There is a note of finality in his judgments that amazes, an infallibility that amuses," writes Vernon L. Parrington. "The Reverend Jonathan frankly acknowledges himself to be the boon companion of Reason, the favored suitor of Truth—from them only has he taken instruction and in their name he professes to speak."

Odell's preferred method of unifying political opinion was to hang everybody who disagreed with him:

> At length the day of Vengeance is at hand:
> The exterminating Angel takes his stand:
> Hear the last summons, rebels, and relent:
> Yet but a moment is there to repent.

He kept an enemies list that sounds sublimely impartial, but only because he hated Federalists and republicans with equal venom. Washington, Adams, Jefferson, Morris, Paine, and just about everybody else in the American pantheon was plunged into a bath of sulphurous ink:

> Ask I too much? then grant me for a time
> Some deleterious pow'rs of acrid rhyme:
> Some ars'nic verse, to poison with the pen
> These rats, who nestle in the lion's den!

He went on espousing his loyalist views right up to the surrender of Cornwallis. At last, when independence was a fait accompli, he went into voluntary exile in Nova Scotia, where he lived long and sullenly on a pension from the Crown. The slight renown he enjoys today comes mainly from a nickname bestowed on him by a leading authority on the literature of the American Revolution, Moses Coit Tyler, who called him "Toryissimus."

Jonathan Odell is an example of how easily misanthropy can lead to treason. He swam against the tide because he hated the tide, whatever it happened to be. It's a good bet that if he had been a Northerner during the Civil War he would have been a Copperhead, and if he had been a Southerner he would have been a Scallawag, because even his different drummer heard a different drummer.

Mad, bad, and dangerous to know was our Jonathan, yet I can't help feeling that at last I have found Mr. Right. I can see the two of us tucked up together in Nova Scotia, a bundling board between us, watching Alistair Cooke cross his legs and working on our garden of verses.

* * *

"Anonymous" was a woman,
The Libbers all insist.
She never had a by-line,
For she didn't dare exist.

She scribbled Christian verses,
Penned domestic lucubrations,
Stuffed maxims in her cookbook
To express her aggravations.

She ended up in *Bartlett's*
A queen without a throne,
Where everything she ever wrote
Was classified "Unknown."

But then there came a forum
Where she could sign her spleen,
In letters to the editor
Of *MS.*-fits magazine.

She wrote about her vulva
And the joys of getting head,
And described the hell of marriage
When a husband farts in bed.

She sang of masturbation,
Told the Pope to take a hike,

FLORENCE KING

Then listed her abortions
And announced she was a dyke.

But when it came to signatures
Her courage was dispelled,
So the *Bartlett's* of the future
Will call her "Name Withheld."

    *   *   *

Watching Richard Simmons
As he flaps his little hands,
And kicks his hairless legs up high
And sings along with bands,
A fervent picture leaps to mind
And wishful thought enfolds me
As I visualize him sweatin' to
A quintessential oldie.
It's awfully hard to rhyme it—
After all, I'm not a Horace—
But I'd love to see him buggered
By a Rex Tyrannosaurus.

    *   *   *

A famous politician
Approached the mike one day
To face up to his demons
And lay frailties away.

"I need help," he stated bravely,
"I'm bottomed out, done in,
And now I've come to tell you
That the healing must begin."

"The long denial ends today,
I confess to you I'm sick.
The agony is over
But recovery's never quick."

"Out of control for many years,
I let myself get slack,
But now I need your helping hand
As I start the long road back."

The hall was stunned and silent,
You could hear a fallen pin
As every word he uttered
Seemed to touch our hearts within.

We wept with deep emotion,
For we knew he'd hit a skid,
Yet we couldn't help but wonder
Just what it was he did.

We didn't know his substance,
We didn't know his sin,
We didn't even know for sure
What Center he was in.

He never actually named it,
Of light he shed no beam,
But no one dared to question
A search for self-esteem.

He was working through his problems,
Being counseled for abuse,
And anyone who doubted it
Was hopelessly obtuse.

FLORENCE KING

He was dancing to the 12-step,
That was fundamental,
And anyone who looked askance
Was nothing but judgmental.

We told ourselves with great relief
That nothing mattered but belief.
We offered him our hopes and tears
And prayed that he was with his peers:

"Ask Betty Ford to kiss him, Lord,
Ask Liz to make him well,
Let Skitty Kitty Detoxis
Share with him her hell."

At some point in his absence
Came a startling discovery:
We had scrapped the national anthem
To sing "We're In Recovery."

He came back home to cheering throngs
Whose deepest needs he met
When he said, "I offer nothing
But blood tests, spoils, and sweat."

He wept on Sally Jessy,
And Oprah hugged his pain
When he said he had a habit
Of snorting up cocaine.

He slapped a high five with Sonya Live,
And confessed he had really botched it,
He said a prayer on MacNeil and Lehrer
And for once somebody watched it.

"Larry, I'm no human being,"
"Phil, I'm beyond the pale,
"I've nowhere to go and I've sunk so low
That I might as well be a white male."

The U.S. Constitution
Has no anchor, just a sail,
So it wasn't any wonder
That he hit the campaign trail.

He got elected as expected
And what do you suppose?
Everyone knew but none would say
"The President has no nose."

*   *   *

A Nineties man sat drinking
And tried to do some thinking
But the woman on the barstool hurled her flak.
She talked of her agenda
And the needs of her pudenda
And why she wouldn't ride the Mommy Track.
She said, "Now, you see here, if I gave up my career
I would be a little nothing on the shelf.
I would suffocate and smother being just a wife and
    mother,
I need options and a lifestyle for myself."
Her husband turned around
To escape the steady sound
But her manifesto carried to great lengths.
She talked of her profession
And the value of aggression

And why she wouldn't give up female strengths.
He said, "This chick is sick," then he heard a little *click!*
Now he knew exactly what was wrong.
He kicked her in the tushie and she fell into the sushi,
Then he stood up on the bar and sang a song:

"I want a girl just like the girl
That majored in Home Ec.
She loved to cook, never read a book
Nor even wrote a check.
With her I wouldn't need paternal leave,
She had no career ambitions up her sleeve,
That's why I want a girl just like the girl
That majored in Home Ec."

        *   *   *

One night while watching "Crossfire"
In the privacy of home,
I fell asleep and woke up in
A show called "Twilight Zone."

The Lib Flit started leaking
From a ceiling vent o'erspread,
And in a flash it melted down
That tiny little head.

Next the scrawny chicken neck,
And then the bony chest
Had vanished in an acid bath
As quickly as the rest.

The end was not long coming,
Though it was a little crass.

A fer-de-lance slid through the stage
And bit him in the ass.

The long snide night was over,
He would pass this way no more.
Obnoxious Michael Kinsley
Was a grease spot on the floor.

BIBLIOGRAPHY

When I got the first tenuous idea for this book more than a decade ago, I began to gear my private reading along lines likely to result in a steadily increasing knowledge of misanthropy without actually Doing Research, which I hate: going to college once is one time too many, in my opinion.

I also tried to influence my reviewing assignments in the same way, which produced a memorable office exchange that I overheard while waiting on the phone.

"Florence is interested in misanthropes."

"So what else is new?"

Several of my book editors came through, bless them. In fact, I had them so well-trained that one called up and simply said, "I've got one here about a real shit so I thought of you." (Never let the intellectuals bamboozle you into thinking that the field of literary criticism is any more of an Arcadian glade than life's other fields.)

192

WITH CHARITY TOWARD NONE

I proceeded in my own fashion, writing down everything that appealed to me in my quotations notebook, which is always at my side whenever I read; scribbling my original ideas on pieces of scratch paper and tossing them in a file marked *Misan;* and reading and clipping both Washington papers and my own local paper every day.

The following list is not complete by any means. I have read hundreds of books over the last ten years, and bits and pieces of hundreds more, but these are the ones I read or reread in the last year or so while outlining and writing *With Charity Toward None.* I have starred those I particularly enjoyed and recommend for general reading.

Adams, Henry *The Letters of Henry Adams, 1858–1891*
Adams, Henry *The Education of Henry Adams*
Alexander, Charles C. *Ty Cobb*
Ames, Fisher *Works of Fisher Ames.* W. B. Allen, ed.
*Babbitt, Irving *Democracy and Leadership*
*Babbitt, Irving *Rousseau and Romanticism*
*Bergreen, Laurence *As Thousands Cheer: The Life of Irving Berlin*
Boswell, James *Boswell on the Grand Tour: Germany and Switzerland, 1764.*
     Frederick A. Pottle, ed.
*Branden, Barbara *The Passion of Ayn Rand*
*Cecil, Henry. *Daughters in Law*
Cerf, Barry *Anatole France: The Degeneration of a Great Writer*
Cooper, James Fenimore *The American Democrat*
Drabble, Margaret, ed. *Oxford Companion to English Literature*
Durant, Will *Rousseau and Revolution*
Durant, Will *The Age of Voltaire*
Elder, Donald *Ring Lardner*
Fecher, Charles A., ed. *The Diary of H.L. Mencken*
Geismar, Maxwell *Writers in Crisis*
Gerber, John C. *Mark Twain*
*Kirk Russell, ed. *The Portable Conservative Reader*
Lardner, Ring *Gullible's Travels, Etc.*
*Leider, Emily Wortis *California's Daughter: Gertrude Atherton and Her Times*
*Liddy, G. Gordon *Will*
*Loomis, Stanley *Paris in the Terror*
*Loomis, Stanley *Du Barry*
McCallum, John *The Tiger Wore Spikes*

FLORENCE KING

McCarthy, Patrick *Céline*
Molière *Le Misanthrope.* Richard Wilbur translation.
Nixon, Richard M. *Six Crises*
O'Connell, David *Louis-Ferdinand Céline*
*O'Connor, Richard *Ambrose Bierce: A Biography*
*O'Toole, Patricia *The Five of Hearts: An Intimate Portrait of Henry Adams and His Friends, 1880–1918*
Parrington, Vernon L. *Main Currents in American Thought*
Patrick, Walton R. *Ring Lardner*
Pobedonostsev, Konstantin *Reflections of a Russian Statesman.* Foreword by Murray Polner
Rostand, Edmond *Cyrano de Bergerac.* Brian Hooker translation
*Schama, Simon *Citizens*
Starkie, Enid. *Flaubert: The Making of the Master*
Steegmuller, Francis. *Flaubert and Madame Bovary*
Twain, Mark *Letters From the Earth.* Bernard DeVoto, ed.
Twain, Mark "The Man Who Corrupted Hadleysburg"
Untermeyer, Louis *Makers of the Modern World*
Vicinus, Martha and Nergaard, Bea, eds. *Ever Yours, Florence Nightingale: Selected Letters.*

194